Mediterranean Diet Cookbook for Beginners

1800 Days of Healthy, Easy, Delicious, and Nutritious Recipes for Fast & Healthy Meals. Includes a 28-Day Meal Plan to Build a Healthier Eating Lifestyle

Amanda Ray

© Copyright 2024 - All rights reserved.

The content contained within this book may not be reproduced, duplicated, or transmitted without direct written permission from the author or publisher.

Under no circumstances will any blame or legal responsibility be held against the publisher or author for any damages, reparations, or monetary losses due to the information contained within this book, either directly or indirectly.

Legal Notice:

This book is copyright-protected. It is only for personal use. You cannot amend, distribute, sell, use, quote, or paraphrase any part or the content within it without the consent of the author or publisher.

Disclaimer Notice:

Please note that the information contained within this document is for educational and entertainment purposes only. All efforts have been made to present accurate, up-to-date, reliable, and complete information. No warranties of any kind are declared or implied. Readers acknowledge that the author is not engaged in rendering legal, financial, medical, or professional advice. The content within this book has been derived from various sources. Please consult a licensed professional before attempting any techniques outlined in this book.

By reading this document, the reader agrees that under no circumstances is the author responsible for any direct or indirect losses incurred as a result of the use of the information contained within this document, including, but not limited to, errors, omissions, or inaccuracies.

Table of Content

Introduction 7

Chapter 1: About the Mediterranean Diet 9
What is the Mediterranean Diet? 9
Mediterranean Diet vs Other Diets 9
The Mediterranean Diet Pyramid 10
What to eat in the Mediterranean Diet? 11
What to avoid in the Mediterranean Diet? 12
How effective is it in reducing blood pressure? 12
Mediterranean Diet for Weight Loss 12
FAQ Mediterranean Diet 13
Shopping List.. 13

Chapter 2: Breakfast Recipes 15
Greek Yogurt Parfait with Honey and Berries... 15
Mediterranean Breakfast Wrap 15
Lemon Ricotta Pancakes with Blueberries 16
Turkish Menemen with Bell Peppers............. 17
Mediterranean Egg Muffins with Zucchini and Sun-dried Tomatoes....................................... 17
Cilbir: Turkish Poached Eggs with Yogurt Sauce... 18
Israeli Sabich Sandwich 19
Greek Avocado Toast with Kalamata Olives 20

Greek Spinach and Feta Pie (Spanakopita) ...20
Mediterranean Overnight Oats with Apricots and Pistachios.. 21

Chapter 3: Appetizers and Snacks..23
Hummus and Veggie Sticks 23
Tzatziki Dip 24
Mediterranean Bruschetta 24
Greek Salad Skewers 25
Marinated Olives 25
Caponata Crostini...26
Spinach and Feta Stuffed Mushrooms...........27
Falafel Bites 27
Muhammara..28

Chapter 4: Salads and Sides Dishes 29
Chickpea and Roasted Pepper Salad..............29
Mediterranean Beet Salad..............................30
Fennel and Orange Salad 30
Tabbouleh... 31
Roasted Red Pepper and Feta Spread........... 31
Baba Ganoush 32
Marinated Olives and Feta 32
Cucumber Yogurt Salad (Tzatziki) 33
Za'atar Roasted Carrots..................................34

Lemon Herb Orzo Salad 34

Chapter 5: Soups and Stew Recipes 36

Lentil and Spinach Soup 36

Chickpea and Rosemary Soup 36

Tomato and Basil Soup 37

Mediterranean Fish Stew 38

Greek Lemon Chicken Soup (Avgolemono) ..38

Turkish Red Lentil Soup 39

Mediterranean Vegetable Soup 40

Escarole and White Bean Soup 40

Cretan Tomato Soup with Orzo 41

Gazpacho 42

Chapter 6: Pasta, Pizza, Rice, Pies Recipes 43

Pesto Fusilli with Cherry Tomatoes 43

Creamy Spinach and Mushroom Linguine 43

Tomato and Mozzarella Farfalle 44

Margherita Flatbread Pizza 45

Mediterranean Veggie Pizza 45

Chicken and Pesto Pizza 46

Lemon and Herb Risotto 47

Saffron and Vegetable Pilaf 48

Tomato and Olive Rice Salad 48

Zucchini and Ricotta Galette 49

Chapter 7: Vegetables and Beans ...50

Garlic Sautéed Green Beans 50

Chickpea and Spinach Stew 50

Eggplant and Bell Pepper Caponata 51

Lentil and Roasted Carrot Salad 52

Mediterranean Cucumber and Tomato Salad 52

Stuffed Bell Peppers with Quinoa and Feta ...53

Braised Cannellini Beans with Kale 54

Roasted Broccoli with Lemon and Garlic 54

Zucchini Ribbons with Black Olives and Mint 55

Chard and Potato Gratin 55

Chapter 8: Fish and Shellfish Recipes 57

Garlic Lemon Herb Grilled Salmon 57

Mediterranean Tuna Salad 57

Baked Tilapia with Tomatoes and Olives 58

Easy Cod in Tomato Basil Sauce 59

Mussels in White Wine and Garlic Sauce 59

Olive and Caper Anchovy Pasta 60

Baked Sardines with Lemon and Oregano 60

Seared Scallops with Fennel Salad 61

Mediterranean Fish Stew with Potatoes and Olives 62

Greek-style Shrimp Pasta.............................62

Chapter 9: Poultry Recipes............64

Greek Lemon Chicken Soup (Avgolemono) ..64

Chicken Kebabs with Tzatziki Sauce.............65

Chicken Tagine with Apricots and Almonds..65

Tuscan Chicken with Tomatoes and Spinach 66

Spiced Chicken with Couscous Salad............67

Mediterranean Turkey Burgers.....................68

Chicken Shawarma Wraps 68

Lemon Olive Chicken Thighs 69

Garlic Rosemary Roasted Chicken.................69

Mediterranean Chicken Salad with Olives and Feta 70

Chapter 10: Beef, Pork, Lamb Recipes 72

Grilled Lamb Chops with Mint Sauce 72

Beef and Eggplant Moussaka 73

Mediterranean Pork Tenderloin with Olives and

Feta 73
Lamb Tagine with Dates and Cinnamon 74
Beef Kofta with Yogurt Sauce..........................75
Greek-style Stuffed Bell Peppers with Ground Lamb..75
Spiced Pork Kebabs with Cucumber Salad....76
Mediterranean Beef Stew with Rosemary and Tomatoes 77
Lamb and Spinach Curry 77
Slow-cooked Pork Shoulder with Mediterranean Herbs..78

Chapter 11: Desserts, Fruits Recipes 80
Greek Yogurt with Honey and Walnuts........ 80
Mediterranean Lemon Olive Oil Cake 80
Fresh Fruit Salad with Mint and Lemon Drizzle 81
Baklava Rolls with Pistachio and Honey 82
Mediterranean Almond Cookies 82
Apricot and Almond Tart 83
Fig and Walnut Halva 84
Orange and Rose Water Sorbet.......................84
Mediterranean Date Balls with Coconut........85
Pistachio Pudding with Saffron.......................85

Chapter 12: Beverages 87
Mint and Cucumber Infused Water 87
Mediterranean Iced Coffee with Almond Milk...87
Fresh Pomegranate and Orange Juice.......... 88
Greek Mountain Tea with Lemon and Honey 88
Sparkling Rosemary Limeade 89
Mediterranean Herbal Tea Blend 89
Iced Hibiscus and Rose Tea 90
Lemon and Mint Cooler 91
Olive Leaf Tea 91
Greek Frappe Coffee...92

Chapter 13: Bonus 93
DASH Herb-Baked Chicken Breasts.............93
Quinoa & Vegetable Medley Salad 93
Spinach and Feta Stuffed Tilapia 94
DASH-friendly Whole Wheat Spaghetti with Fresh Tomato Sauce 95
Almond Berry Overnight Oats 95
Slow-Cooked Lentil Soup with Vegetables ...96
Honey Garlic Chicken with Carrots and Broccoli..96
Crockpot Vegetable and Bean Chili 97
Savory Pot Roast with Root Vegetables.........97
Creamy Butternut Squash Soup.....................98
Air-Fried Parmesan Zucchini Sticks 99
Crispy Air Fryer Lemon Pepper Chicken Wings...99
Golden-Brown Air Fryer Potato Wedges 100
Air Fryer Coconut Shrimp with Dipping Sauce...100
Light & Fluffy Air Fryer Donuts 101

Chapter 14: 30-Day Meal Prep Plan 103
Week 1..103
Week 2...104
Week 3...106
Week 4...108

Free Gift..................................... 111
Conclusion outline 112
References 113
Appendix 1: Measurement Conversion Chart 114
Appendix 2: Index Recipes 115
A...115
B...115
C...115
D...116

F	116
G	116
H	117
K	117
L	117
M	118
O	118
P	118
Q	119
R	119
S	120
T	120
W	120
Z	120

Notes..................120

Introduction

Introduction to the Mediterranean Diet Cookbook for Beginners

Are you on a journey to transform your physical and mental health? Are you searching for a dietary path that isn't just a fleeting trend but an age-old, sustainable, and delicious way of living? If the idea of savoring sun-kissed flavors while nourishing your body speaks to you, then the Mediterranean diet is your answer.

The Mediterranean region, renowned for its rich history and diverse cultures, also holds the secrets to one of the healthiest dietary patterns in the world. Rooted in the traditional cuisines of countries along the Mediterranean coast, this diet is not just about weight management; it's a holistic approach to better health, longevity, and a joyful relationship with food.

The Mediterranean diet is not merely a list of dos and don'ts. Instead, it paints a colorful palette of foods ranging from fresh fruits, vegetables, whole grains, and olive oil to moderate portions of poultry, fish, and wine. This dietary journey is as much about indulging in the pleasures of natural flavors as it is about promoting heart health, stable blood sugar, and overall well-being.

Greetings, I am Winona Bax, and my journey with the Mediterranean diet started many moons ago. Like many, I searched for a dietary regime that was both beneficial and enjoyable. The Mediterranean diet, with its balance of flavors and nutrients, was a revelation to me. My countless hours in understanding, experimenting, and relishing this diet have reshaped my relationship with food and health. It's my mission to help you embark on this transformative journey, too.

This book serves as your compass, guiding you through the rich tapestry of the Mediterranean diet. It breaks down its principles and manifold benefits. It provides a bounty of recipes that capture the essence of the Mediterranean spirit. Divided thoughtfully into sections, you'll find everything from breakfast to dinner, including delightful snacks, vegetarian and vegan delights, and sumptuous desserts that will satiate without weighing you down. To simplify your transition, we've also curated a sample four-week meal plan, helping you integrate this diet seamlessly into your daily life.

So, are you ready to set sail on a culinary voyage that promises tantalizing tastes and a treasure trove of health benefits? Let's embark on this Mediterranean journey together, savoring each bite and celebrating every health milestone. Welcome to the Mediterranean Diet Cookbook for Beginners.

Greetings! My name is Amanda Ray, and I am a seasoned cookbook author with extensive expertise in the culinary world. I wanted to thank you for grabbing a copy of my diet cookbook. Your support means the world to me.

Creating this cookbook was an actual passion project for me. I wanted to make something that tastes amazing and helps people care for their health better. It's all about making those small steps towards a healthier lifestyle, and having you on board makes it all worthwhile.

I've put a lot of heart and soul into crafting these recipes, knowing how important it is to make healthy eating delicious and accessible. With so many health issues cropping up at younger ages, paying attention to what we eat is more crucial than ever.

Your decision to try out the recipes in this cookbook is a vote of confidence in my mission, and I'm genuinely grateful for that. I hope you enjoy cooking and eating from it as much as I enjoyed putting it together.

I'd love to hear your thoughts on the cookbook if you have a spare moment. Your feedback could be super helpful for others thinking about giving it a try. Just a few words from you could make a big difference in someone else's decision-making process.

Just 3 easy steps to share your thoughts:

1. Head over to Your Orders.

2. Click «Write a product review» in the Customer Reviews section.

3. Choose a rating, and feel free to add any text, photos, or videos you'd like. Then, hit Submit!

Once again, thank you so much for your support and trust. I hope this cookbook brings you extra joy and health.

Chapter 1: About the Mediterranean Diet

What is the Mediterranean Diet?

The Mediterranean Diet is a dietary approach that follows the traditional eating patterns of countries surrounding the Mediterranean Sea. This diet is considered one of the healthiest globally. It has resulted in numerous favorable health impacts, such as reducing the risk of heart disease, stroke, and other malignancies. The Mediterranean diet comprises a range of foods, including legumes, whole grains, fruits, vegetables, nuts, seeds, and olive oil.

The dish includes minor quantities of dairy, small portions of red meat, and moderate servings of fish and fowl. The diet is rich in fiber, phytochemicals (natural compounds found in plants that have been shown to have health benefits), and antioxidants while being low in trans fat, saturated fat, and processed carbohydrates. A vital component of the Mediterranean diet is olive oil. The monounsaturated fats in this oil can lower LDL cholesterol levels and decrease the risk of heart disease. Olive oil is rich in vitamin E.It is an antioxidant that may aid in preventing cancer and other chronic diseases. Fish is a vital component of the Mediterranean diet. Omega-3 fatty acids in fish can lower inflammation and lessen the risk of heart disease, stroke, and other diseases. The Mediterranean diet includes poultry, eggs, protein-rich foods, and minerals. Fruits and vegetables predominate in the Mediterranean diet. Rich in fiber, vitamins, and minerals, these foods have minimal calories.

The Mediterranean Diet is both healthy and environmentally sustainable. The diet focuses on consuming whole, less processed foods sourced from local farmers and in season. In the process, the environmental impact of food production can be decreased, and local farmers and food systems can be strengthened. The Mediterranean diet is nourishing and long-lasting, a dietary pattern with many health benefits. The Mediterranean Diet is a nutritious, enduring dietary pattern with numerous health advantages.

The diet includes moderate quantities of fish, chicken, and dairy items. The diet consists of whole grains, fruits, vegetables, legumes, nuts, seeds, and olive oil. Fruits and vegetables include antioxidants and phytochemicals that may help prevent cancer and other chronic diseases.

The diet is rich in fiber, phytochemicals, and antioxidants while being low in trans fat, saturated fat, and processed carbohydrates. Consuming a Mediterranean diet can help sustain environmentally friendly food systems with long-term viability. They can enhance their well-being and reduce their susceptibility to chronic illnesses.

Mediterranean Diet vs Other Diets

The Mediterranean diet is frequently compared to the Western, Paleo, and ketogenic diets. The Mediterranean diet is known to have numerous health advantages.

The Mediterranean Diet is rich in whole, minimally processed foods and low in saturated fat and added sugars, unlike the Western Diet, which consists of significant amounts of processed foods, red and processed meats, and sugary drinks. Therefore, individuals looking to improve their overall health and reduce their risk of chronic diseases may find the Mediterranean Diet beneficial.

The Paleo and Mediterranean diets emphasize consuming complete, unadulterated foods while avoiding grains, legumes, and dairy products. The Mediterranean Diet includes whole grains, legumes, and dairy products, which provide essential nutrients and fiber that may be deficient in a rigorous Paleo diet.

The Ketogenic diet promotes weight loss and addresses some health conditions. It involves consuming high fat, moderate protein, and low carbs. The Mediterranean Diet encourages a balanced diet with nutrient-rich foods such as whole grains, fruits, and vegetables.

The Mediterranean Diet offers numerous health benefits and is a nutritious and enduring dietary regimen. The Mediterranean Diet prioritizes whole, less processed foods. Although there are some similarities, this diet has a more optimal balance of macronutrient ratios than other diets. Opting for the Mediterranean Diet is prudent for anyone seeking to enhance their overall health and reduce the risk of chronic diseases.

The Mediterranean Diet Pyramid

The Mediterranean Diet Pyramid illustrates the typical dietary habits of individuals residing in nations bordering the Mediterranean Sea. The Mediterranean Diet Foundation and the Harvard School of Public Health collaborated to create a pyramid to guide individuals to adhere to the Mediterranean Diet.

Physical activity and social connections are foundational elements crucial for a healthy lifestyle. This level comprises whole grains, fruits, vegetables, legumes, nuts, and seeds, which are the fundamental components of the Mediterranean diet.

Fish, seafood, poultry, eggs, and dairy products belong to this category and should be consumed in moderation. Red meat and sweets at the top of the pyramid should be consumed in moderation.

Olive oil is essential in the Mediterranean Diet. A little cup placed beside the pyramid indicates that it should be used in moderation.

The Mediterranean Diet Pyramid emphasizes water as the optimal beverage choice, advising individuals to consume less alcohol and sugary beverages.

The Mediterranean Diet Pyramid provides a structured guide for individuals interested in adhering to the Mediterranean Diet.

Consuming foods from the Mediterranean Food Pyramid can help people lead healthier lives and reduce the risk of developing chronic diseases.

Advantages of the Mediterranean Diet

The Mediterranean Diet is recognized for its numerous health benefits and is a wholesome dietary approach. The diet's advantages include:

- **Lowering the likelihood of heart disease:** The diet's inclusion of healthy fats, specifically monounsaturated and polyunsaturated fats, has been shown to reduce LDL cholesterol levels, thereby diminishing the risk of heart disease.
- **Enhancing mental function:** The diet contains high levels of antioxidants and anti-inflammatory compounds linked to enhanced cognitive function and a lower likelihood of developing Alzheimer's disease and other neurodegenerative conditions.

- **Decreasing cancer risk:** A diet abundant in fruits, vegetables, whole grains, and legumes provides fiber, antioxidants, and phytonutrients that may contribute to the prevention of various cancers, including those of the colon, breast, and prostate.
- **Lowering the risk of type 2 diabetes:** By limiting refined sugars and carbohydrates, the Mediterranean diet helps prevent insulin resistance and reduces the risk of developing type 2 diabetes.
- **Aiding in weight management:** Focusing on whole foods and minimally processed items, along with a balanced intake of healthy fats, supports maintaining a healthy weight and reduces the likelihood of obesity.
- **Promoting digestive health:** The diet is high in fiber, prebiotics, and probiotics, and it supports digestive health and may lower the risk of conditions such as inflammatory bowel disease and irritable bowel syndrome.
- **Environmental sustainability:** The diet emphasizes seasonal and locally sourced produce along with minimally processed foods, promoting environmental sustainability and reducing food production's ecological impact.

The Mediterranean Diet is a sustainable and health-promoting eating pattern that can enhance general health, reduce the risk of chronic diseases, and promote environmentally friendly and enduring food systems.

What to eat in the Mediterranean Diet?

Most likely, the Mediterranean Diet draws on the traditional eating patterns of people from regions surrounding the Mediterranean Sea. It promotes a balance of macronutrients, focusing on healthy fats, carbohydrates, and proteins, and emphasizes the consumption of whole, minimally processed foods. Key components of the Mediterranean Diet include:

- **Whole grains:** Foods such as whole-grain bread, pasta, and cereals are staples in the Mediterranean diet, providing sustained energy and being rich in fiber, vitamins, and minerals.
- **Fruits and vegetables:** A wide array of fruits and vegetables, including leafy greens, tomatoes, peppers, and citrus fruits, are central to the diet, offering essential nutrients and antioxidants for health.
- **Legumes:** Foods like chickpeas, lentils, and beans are excellent sources of fiber, complex carbohydrates, and protein and can be used in various dishes, from soups to salads.
- **Nuts and seeds:** These are important for their protein, fiber, and healthy fats and can be enjoyed as snacks or added to dishes for extra flavor and nutritional value.
- **Fish and seafood:** The diet emphasizes consuming fish and seafood, which are high in omega-3 fatty acids known for their anti-inflammatory properties and benefits to heart health.
- **Olive oil:** As a primary source of fat, olive oil is extensively used in the Mediterranean diet instead of other fats like butter, providing monounsaturated fats that are beneficial for heart health and can help reduce inflammation.

Individuals can embrace the Mediterranean Diet and its numerous health benefits by incorporating these foods into their diet.

What to avoid in the Mediterranean Diet?

The Mediterranean Diet, inspired by the traditional dietary habits of those living near the Mediterranean Sea, emphasizes a balanced intake of macronutrients and focuses on whole, lightly processed foods. Key elements of this diet include:

- Whole grains like bread, pasta, and cereal made from whole grains offer sustained energy and are rich in fiber, vitamins, and minerals.
- < UNK> Various fruits and vegetables, like leafy greens, tomatoes, peppers, and citrus, are pivotal for their nutrient and antioxidant content.
- Legumes, including chickpeas, lentils, and beans, valued for their fiber, complex carbohydrates, and protein, are versatile in dishes from soups to salads.
- Nuts and seeds offer protein, fiber, and healthy fats and are suitable as snacks or as additions to enhance flavor and nutrition in meals.
- Fish and seafood, which are central to the diet for their omega-3 fatty acids, are known to reduce inflammation and support heart health.
- Olive oil, the main source of fat in the diet, is chosen over other fats like butter due to its monounsaturated fats known to be heart-healthy and anti-inflammatory.

How effective is it in reducing blood pressure?

The Mediterranean diet reduces blood pressure, a major risk factor for heart disease and stroke. Research has demonstrated that the Mediterranean Diet can lower both systolic and diastolic blood pressure in individuals with hypertension.

Overweight and obese patients with metabolic syndrome who adhered to the Mediterranean Diet for two years experienced decreased systolic and diastolic blood pressure, as reported by The American Journal of Clinical Nutrition. Another study published in JAMA found that adopting the Mediterranean Diet for six months led to reduced blood pressure in untreated individuals with hypertension.

The Mediterranean diet, which focuses on natural, minimally processed foods and healthy fats such as olive oil, can reduce blood pressure. The exact mechanism, however, remains obscure. The Mediterranean diet includes salt and potassium, and it has the benefit of reducing blood pressure.

The Mediterranean Diet reduces blood pressure and enhances cardiovascular well-being. Individuals with hypertension might decrease their chances of developing heart disease and stroke by adhering to the Mediterranean Diet, which also aids in reducing blood pressure.

Mediterranean Diet for Weight Loss

The Mediterranean Diet is nutritious and can facilitate weight loss. The Mediterranean Diet helps facilitate healthy weight reduction.

The Mediterranean Diet focuses on whole, minimally processed foods rich in fiber, protein, and healthy fats while being low in saturated fat and added sugars. These foods offer sustained energy and help reduce hunger and cravings, which can assist in weight loss.

The Mediterranean Diet advocates for physical activity to aid with weight loss. The diet promotes social interaction and stress management, which might assist individuals in overcoming emotional eating and other unhealthy behaviors.

Various investigations have demonstrated the effectiveness of the Mediterranean Diet for weight loss. According to The New England Journal of Medicine, individuals adhering to the Mediterranean Diet experienced more weight loss than those following a low-fat diet. The Mediterranean Diet was effective for sustained weight loss and management in a recent trial published in the American Journal of Clinical Nutrition.

The Mediterranean Diet, emphasizing whole, minimally processed foods and a balanced macronutrient intake, can facilitate weight loss. People can safely reduce their weight and improve their health by following the Mediterranean Diet.

FAQ Mediterranean Diet

Q: Can the Mediterranean diet accommodate vegetarian and vegan lifestyles?

A: The Mediterranean Diet dietbe modified to fit vegetarian and vegan lifestyles. It focuses on various unprocessed plant foods, including abundant fruits, vegetables, beans, nuts, and seeds. It allows for the inclusion of modest quantities of dairy and eggs for those who consume them.

Q: Is adhering to the Mediterranean diet considered expensive?

A: The Mediterranean diet can be cost-effective because it emphasizes unprocessed, whole foods widely available at local supermarkets. It encourages the consumption of locally sourced and in-season produce, often more affordable than out-of-season or imported items.

Q: Is the Mediterranean diet sustainable over the long term?

A: The Mediterranean Diet is designed for long-term adherence, promoting a well-rounded intake of macronutrients and focusing on whole and minimally processed foods. It also strongly emphasizes lifestyle factors such as managing stress, engaging in social activities, and regular physical activity, which contribute to overall health and longevity.

Q: Is the Mediterranean diet suitable for individuals with existing health conditions?

A: Most individuals, including those with health conditions such as heart disease, type 2 diabetes, and hypertension, can safely follow and benefit from the Mediterranean diet. Nonetheless, individuals with specific health concerns should consult their healthcare provider before making significant dietary changes.

Shopping List

A standard grocery list for someone adhering to the Mediterranean Diet includes the following items:

Examples of whole grains include oats, brown rice, quinoa, whole wheat bread, pasta, and breadsticks.

Green leafy vegetables, tomatoes, peppers, onions, garlic, broccoli, carrots, berries, apples, oranges, and grapes are among the fruits and vegetables that are accessible.

Legumes consist of kidney beans, black beans, lentils, and chickpeas.

Almonds, walnuts, cashews, pumpkin seeds, and chia seeds are examples of nuts and seeds.

Salmon, tuna, shrimp, and mussels are examples of seafood.

Chickens and turkeys are both classified as poultry.

Our dairy products include Greek yogurt, feta cheese, and Parmesan cheese.

It is advisable to use extra-virgin olive oil to cook and make salad dressings.

Basil, oregano, parsley, rosemary, thyme, and cumin are often used herbs and spices.

The drinks included red wine, herbal tea, and water in moderation.

When shopping for the Mediterranean Diet, choose whole, minimally processed foods and avoid highly processed, sugary meals. To promote sustainable and eco-friendly food systems, customers should choose locally grown produce that is in season wherever possible.

Chapter 2: Breakfast Recipes

Greek Yogurt Parfait with Honey and Berries

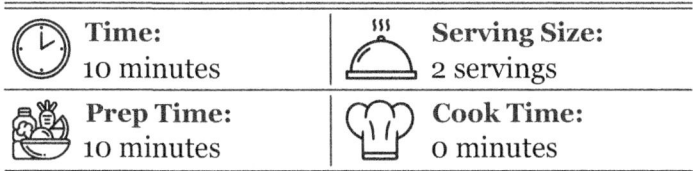

Nutritional Facts Per Serving (1 parfait):

Calories: 235, Fat: 5g, Total Carbohydrate: 34g, Protein: 15g, Sodium: 70mg.

Ingredients:

- 2 cups Greek yogurt (non-fat or low-fat)
- 1 cup mixed berries (e.g., strawberries, blueberries, raspberries, blackberries)
- 4 tablespoons honey
- 1/4 cup granola
- 1/4 cup chopped nuts (e.g., almonds, walnuts, or pistachios)
- 2 teaspoons chia seeds (optional)
- 2 sprigs of mint for garnish (optional)

Directions:

1. Start by layering 1/2 cup of Greek yogurt in two parfait glasses or clear bowls in each glass.
2. Add 1/4 cup of mixed berries to the yogurt layer in each glass.
3. Drizzle 1 tablespoon of honey over the berries in each glass.
4. Sprinkle 2 tablespoons of granola and 2 tablespoons of chopped nuts in each glass.
5. Add another 1/2 cup of Greek yogurt, 1/4 cup of mixed berries, 1 tablespoon of honey, and the rest of the granola and chopped nuts to each glass to continue the layering process.
6. If desired, sprinkle chia seeds on top of each parfait for added texture and nutrition.
7. If preferred, garnish with a mint sprig before serving. Enjoy your healthy and mouthwatering Greek yogurt parfait with honey and berries.

Mediterranean Breakfast Wrap

Time: 20 minutes	Serving Size: 4 tortillaas
Prep Time: 15 minutes	Cook Time: 5 minutes

Nutritional Facts Per Serving (1 wrap):

Calories: 375, Fat: 20g, Total Carbohydrate: 32g, Protein: 18g, Sodium: 600mg.

Ingredients:

- 4 large whole wheat tortillas or wraps
- 4 large eggs

- 1 tablespoon olive oil
- 1/2 medium onion, chopped
- 1 small bell pepper (red, yellow, or orange), chopped
- 1/2 cup cherry tomatoes, halved
- 1/2 cup baby spinach, roughly chopped
- 1/2 cup crumbled feta cheese
- 1/4 cup kalamata olives, pitted and chopped
- 1/2 teaspoon dried oregano
- Salt and black pepper, to taste
- Optional: tzatziki sauce or hummus for spreading

Directions:

1. Heat your grill or oven grill to a temperature of medium-high.
2. Cherry tomatoes, chopped basil, red onion, minced garlic, 2 tablespoons extra virgin olive oil, balsamic vinegar, salt, and black pepper should all be incorporated in a large mixing basin. Once fully connected, leave to marinate for at least ten minutes.
3. Slices of bread can be prepared by placing them directly on the grill or a baking tray. Use the remaining tablespoon of olive oil to brush each slice of bread.
4. Grill or broil the bread pieces until they are crisp and golden brown, about one to two minutes per side. Keep a watchful eye on them to avoid scorching.
5. After taking the bread pieces out of the grill or oven, let them cool.
6. Evenly distribute the tomatoes and basil on each slice of bread by spooning the marinated tomato mixture over it.
7. Optional: Top each bruschetta piece with shredded Pecorino Romano or Parmesan cheese.
8. Enjoy your Tuscan Tomato Basil Bruschetta right away after serving!

Lemon Ricotta Pancakes with Blueberries

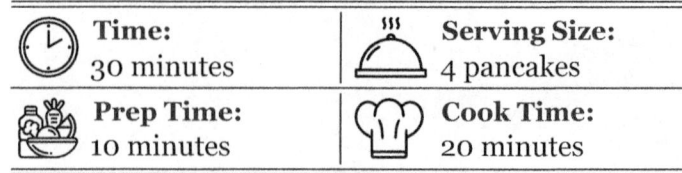

Time: 30 minutes	Serving Size: 4 pancakes
Prep Time: 10 minutes	Cook Time: 20 minutes

Nutritional Facts Per Serving (1 serving):

Calories: 385, Fat: 15g, Total Carbohydrate: 47g, Protein: 17g, Sodium: 280mg.

Ingredients:

- 1 1/2 cups all-purpose flour
- 1/4 cup granulated sugar
- 2 teaspoons baking powder
- 1/2 teaspoon baking soda
- 1/4 teaspoon salt
- 1 cup whole milk ricotta cheese
- 3/4 cup milk
- 2 large eggs
- 1 tablespoon lemon zest (from 1 large lemon)
- 2 tablespoons fresh lemon juice
- 1 teaspoon pure vanilla extract
- 1 cup fresh blueberries
- Butter or non-stick cooking spray for greasing the pan
- Optional: powdered sugar and maple syrup for serving

Directions:

1. Combine the flour, sugar, baking powder, baking soda, and salt in a big bowl. Take out of the way.
2. Pour the milk, eggs, ricotta cheese, lemon juice, zest, and vanilla extract into a separate bowl. Mix until creamy and smooth.
3. Gently fold in the fresh blueberries. Stir the dry ingredients carefully until incorporated, then slowly add the liquid components. Take

caution if you mix too little.

4. To warm up a big nonstick skillet or griddle, place it over medium heat. Apply a thin layer of butter or nonstick frying spray to the surface.

5. Pour enough batter into the skillet for one pancake. Simmer until bubbles form on top, and the edges look firm for about 1 to 2 minutes. It should be golden brown and fully cooked after the pancake has been baked for two to three minutes on each side.

6. Continue using the remaining batter, adding extra butter or using nonstick cooking spray on the skillet.

7. Serve the pancakes warm with powdered sugar on top and drizzle with maple syrup, if desired. Savor your Pancakes with Blueberries and Ricotta.

Turkish Menemen with Bell Peppers

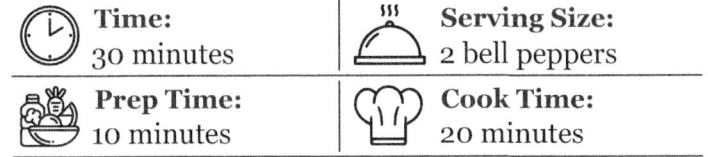

Time: 30 minutes	Serving Size: 2 bell peppers
Prep Time: 10 minutes	Cook Time: 20 minutes

Nutritional Facts Per Serving (1 serving):

Calories: 275, Fat: 20g, Total Carbohydrate: 13g, Protein: 13g, Sodium: 450mg.

Ingredients:

- 2 tablespoons olive oil
- 1 medium onion, finely chopped
- 1 red bell pepper, finely chopped
- 1 green bell pepper, finely chopped
- 3 cloves garlic, minced
- 1 1/2 cups canned crushed tomatoes
- 1 teaspoon paprika
- 1/2 teaspoon ground cumin
- Salt and black pepper, to taste
- 6 large eggs
- 1/4 cup chopped fresh parsley
- Optional: crusty bread, for serving

Directions:

1. In a large skillet over medium heat, warm the olive oil. When the vegetables are cooked and starting to caramelize, add the chopped onion and bell peppers, and simmer for five to seven minutes.

2. Garlic powder should be added and heated until aromatic after a minute.

3. Add black pepper, salt, cumin, paprika, and smashed tomatoes and stir. Cook for 3–4 minutes, or until the mixture thickens slightly.

4. Enough eggs to cover the tomato mixture in a skillet should be cracked. After cooking for 5–7 minutes with a skillet lid on, the eggs should be cooked to your desired doneness.

5. Sprinkle freshly chopped parsley over the skillet after removing it from the heat.

6. With crusty bread for dipping, if preferred, serve the Turkish Menemen with Bell Peppers hot. Pleasure yourself!

Mediterranean Egg Muffins with Zucchini and Sun-dried Tomatoes

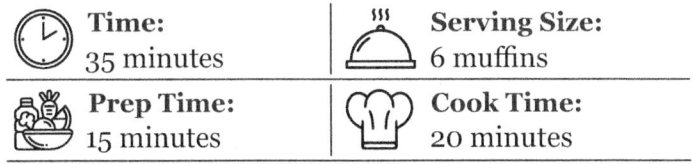

Time: 35 minutes	Serving Size: 6 muffins
Prep Time: 15 minutes	Cook Time: 20 minutes

Nutritional Facts Per Serving (1 muffin):

Calories: 114, Fat: 7g, Total Carbohydrate: 4g, Protein: 8g, Sodium: 210mg.

Ingredients:

- 8 large eggs
- 1/2 cup milk (or

- dairy-free alternative)
- 1/2 teaspoon salt
- 1/4 teaspoon black pepper
- 1 cup shredded zucchini (about 1 medium zucchini)
- 1/2 cup chopped sun-dried tomatoes (packed in oil, drained)
- 1/4 cup chopped fresh basil
- 1/2 cup crumbled feta cheese (or dairy-free alternative)
- 1/4 cup finely chopped red onion
- Non-stick cooking spray

Directions:

1. Preheat your oven to 350°F (180°C) and coat a 12-cup muffin tray with nonstick cooking spray.
2. Whisk together the eggs, milk, pepper, and salt in a large bowl.
3. Squeeze off any excess juice from the shredded zucchini using a clean kitchen towel or piece of paper.
4. Incorporate the chopped red onion, chopped feta cheese, chopped basil, sun-dried tomatoes, and shredded zucchini into the egg mixture. Blend until all components are dispersed equally.
5. Using a large scoop or ladle, fill each of the 12 muffin cups about two-thirds of the way to the top with the egg mixture.
6. Preheat the oven to 200°C. Bake the egg muffins for 20 to 22 minutes, or until they are firm and a toothpick inserted in the center comes out clean.
7. Once removed from the oven, the egg muffins should cool in the tray for five minutes.
8. After carefully removing the egg muffins from the baking pan with a butter knife or tiny spatula, transfer them to a wire rack to cool completely.
9. Serve warm or room temperature Mediterranean Egg Muffins with Sun-Dried Tomatoes and Zucchini. They can be stored in the refrigerator for up to five days in an airtight container, or frozen for up to two months. Use the oven or microwave to warm before serving.
10. Enjoy yourself!

Cilbir: Turkish Poached Eggs with Yogurt Sauce

Time: 30 minutes	Serving Size: 4 poached eggs
Prep Time: 10 minutes	Cook Time: 20 minutes

Nutritional value per serving:

Calories: 324, Fat: 24g, Total carbohydrate content: 8g, Protein: 17g, Sodium: 529 mg.

Ingredients:

- 4 large eggs
- 1 cup of Greek yogurt (or dairy-free alternative)
- 1 clove of garlic, chopped
- 1/2 teaspoon salt to share
- 2 tablespoons of olive oil
- 1 tablespoon unsalted butter
- 1 teaspoon of paprika
- 1/2 teaspoon of red pepper flakes (optional)
- 1 tablespoon of chopped fresh dill
- 1 tablespoon chopped fresh parsley
- 1 teaspoon of white vinegar (for poached eggs)
- freshly ground black pepper, to taste

Directions:

1. In a medium bowl, combine the Greek yogurt, minced garlic, and 1/4 teaspoon salt. Put aside.
2. Three inches of water should be added to a big, shallow saucepan. When the water

is almost boiling, add 1 teaspoon of white vinegar.

3. One egg should crack into a small basin. Place the egg into boiling water carefully. Proceed in the same manner with the remaining eggs, making sure to maintain sufficient space between them to prevent adhesion. Cook for 3 to 4 minutes, or until the eggs are done to your liking, or until the yolk sets. Using a slotted spoon, carefully take the eggs from the water and set them aside to drain on a dish covered with paper towels.

4. In a small saucepan, melt the butter and olive oil over medium heat. For one minute, stir constantly until aromatic. When the butter is melted, add the red pepper and paprika. Take the pan off of the burner.

5. In a small saucepan, cook the butter and olive oil over medium heat. For one minute, stir continuously until aromatic. When the butter is melted, add the red pepper and paprika. Take the pan off of the burner.

6. Present at the table: Serve the yogurt-sauced poached eggs in Turkey with pita bread, crusty bread, or a crisp green salad for a flavorful and nutritious Mediterranean dinner. Have fun!

Israeli Sabich Sandwich

Time: 45 minutes	Serving Size: 4 sandwiches
Prep Time: 20 minutes	Cook Time: 25 minutes

Nutritional Facts Per Serving (1 sandwich):

Calories: 530, Fat: 30g, Total Carbohydrate: 45g, Protein: 18g, Sodium: 968mg.

Ingredients:

- 4 small eggplants sliced into 1/4-inch rounds
- 1/4 cup olive oil
- Salt and black pepper, to taste
- 4 large eggs, hard-boiled and sliced
- 1 cup hummus, store-bought or homemade
- 1/2 cup tahini sauce, store-bought or homemade
- 2 cups Israeli salad (diced cucumber, tomato, and red onion, mixed with lemon juice, olive oil, and salt)
- 1/4 cup chopped fresh parsley
- 1 cup amba sauce, store-bought or homemade (mango-based sauce)
- 4 pita bread pockets

Directions:

1. Set oven temperature to 400°F, or 200°C. Use parchment paper to line a baking sheet.

2. Lay out the aubergine slices on the baking sheet that has been ready. Add salt and pepper to the aubergine and drizzle it with olive oil on both sides. Bake the aubergines for 20 minutes, rotating them halfway through or until they are tender and golden brown.

3. Prepare the Israeli salad by combining chopped cucumber, tomato, and red onion in a medium-sized mixing dish with olive oil, lemon juice, and salt while the aubergine bakes. Once well combined, set away.

4. To assemble the sandwiches, cut a small opening at one end of each pita pocket. Line each pita pocket with about 1/4 cup of hummus, then top with a layer of cooked eggplant slices.

5. Then, top each sandwich with a layer of sliced hard-boiled eggs and a heaping spoonful of Israeli salad. Over the lettuce and egg layers, drizzle the amba sauce and tahini. Garnish with the chopped fresh parsley.

6. Quickly prepare your Israeli Sabich Sandwiches for a tasty and filling Mediterranean lunch, dinner, or even a picnic. Have fun!

Greek Avocado Toast with Kalamata Olives

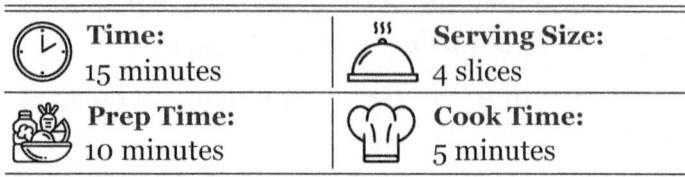

	Time: 15 minutes		Serving Size: 4 slices
	Prep Time: 10 minutes		Cook Time: 5 minutes

Nutritional Facts Per Serving (1 muffin):

Calories: 114, Fat: 7g, Total Carbohydrate: 4g, Protein: 8g, Sodium: 210mg.

Ingredients:

- 4 slices whole grain bread
- 1 ripe avocado, peeled, pitted, and mashed
- 1 clove garlic, minced
- 1 tablespoon lemon juice
- 1 tablespoon extra-virgin olive oil
- Salt and black pepper, to taste
- 1/4 cup pitted and chopped Kalamata olives
- 1/4 cup cherry tomatoes, halved
- 1/4 cup crumbled feta cheese
- 1 tablespoon chopped fresh basil
- 1 tablespoon chopped fresh parsley
- 1/4 teaspoon dried oregano

Directions:

1. In a small bowl, combine the mashed avocado, lemon juice, minced garlic, and olive oil. Season with salt and black pepper to taste. Put aside.
2. Toast the slices of whole grain bread in a toaster or under the broiler until they get the crispiness you like.
3. Spread the avocado mixture evenly over each piece of toasted bread.
4. Even amounts of chopped Kalamata olives, sliced cherry tomato halves, and crumbled feta cheese should be placed on top of each slice.
5. Top each slice with a sprinkling of dried oregano, parsley, and fresh basil.
6. If desired, drizzle with extra virgin olive oil.
7. Enjoy your Greek Avocado Toast with Kalamata Olives right away after serving!
8. Note: You may simply double or treble this meal to feed a larger crowd. As necessary, change the component amounts.

Greek Spinach and Feta Pie (Spanakopita)

	Time: 60 minutes		Serving Size: 6 servings
	Prep Time: 30 minutes		Cook Time: 30 minutes

Nutritional Facts Per Serving (1 serving):

Calories: 355, Fat: 21g, Total Carbohydrate: 27g, Protein: 14g, Sodium: 730mg.

Ingredients:

- 2 tablespoons olive oil
- 1 large onion, chopped
- 2 cloves garlic, minced
- 1 pound fresh spinach, washed, drained, and roughly chopped
- Salt and black pepper, to taste
- 1/2 cup chopped fresh dill
- 1/2 cup chopped fresh parsley
- 8 ounces of feta cheese, crumbled
- 2 large eggs, lightly beaten
- 12 sheets of phyllo dough, thawed
- 1/2 cup unsalted butter, melted

Directions:

1. Set oven temperature to 350°F, or 180°C. Apply nonstick cooking spray to a 9 x 13-inch baking dish.

2. The olive oil should be warmed in a big pan over medium heat. Cook for five minutes, stirring periodically, or until the onion is tender. Add the minced garlic and simmer, stirring frequently, for 30 seconds.

3. Season the skillet with salt and black pepper to taste, and add the chopped spinach. Cook for about 4–5 minutes, or until the spinach wilts. After removing the skillet from the heat, let it cool.

4. In a large bowl, mix together the cooked spinach combination, crumbled feta cheese, chopped fresh parsley and dill, and lightly beaten eggs. Blend thoroughly.

5. To keep the phyllo dough from drying out, cover it with a damp cloth.

6. Line the baking dish with one layer of phyllo dough, allowing the sides to overhang. Spread some melted butter over the phyllo. Apply melted butter to five additional phyllo sheets and repeat this process.

7. Evenly distribute the spinach and feta filling over the phyllo layers.

8. Brush the remaining six phyllo sheets with melted butter and cover the contents.

9. To produce a clean edge, trim the phyllo edges that are overhanging and tuck them around the sides of the dish.

10. Score the upper layers of the phyllo into six equal pieces, taking care not to cut through the filling.

11. Bake the Spanakopita (Greek Spinach and Feta Pie) for 45 to 50 minutes or until the phyllo crust is crisp and golden brown.

12. Allowing the pie to cool for a few minutes, cut it along the scored lines into serving-sized pieces. It is best to serve Spanakopita warm or at room temperature.

Mediterranean Overnight Oats with Apricots and Pistachios

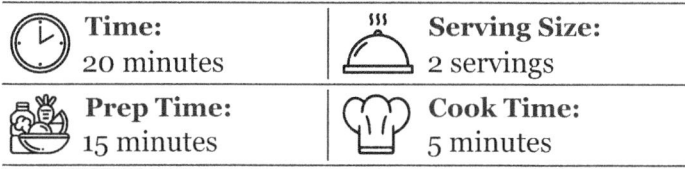

Time: 20 minutes	Serving Size: 2 servings
Prep Time: 15 minutes	Cook Time: 5 minutes

Nutritional Facts Per Serving (1 serving):

Calories: 312, Fat: 12g, Total Carbohydrate: 42g, Protein: 11g, Sodium: 68mg.

Ingredients:

- 1 cup rolled oats
- 2 cups unsweetened almond milk
- 1 cup plain Greek yogurt
- 1 tablespoon honey
- 1 teaspoon ground cinnamon
- 1/2 teaspoon vanilla extract
- 1/4 cup dried apricots, chopped
- 1/4 cup shelled pistachios, roughly chopped
- Pinch of salt
- Optional toppings: additional chopped apricots and pistachios, fresh mint leaves, or a drizzle of honey

Directions:

1. In a large bowl, mix together the rolled oats, almond milk, Greek yogurt, honey, ground cinnamon, and vanilla extract. Until everything is well mixed together.

2. Add the chopped pistachios and dried apricots and fold. To taste, add a small teaspoon of salt.

3. Evenly divide the oat mixture among four

sealed jars or containers. Place a lid on it and chill it for a minimum of eight hours or overnight.

4. Stir the oats thoroughly before serving, and feel free to garnish with more chopped apricots, pistachios, fresh mint leaves, or a honey drizzle.

5. Enjoy your delicious and nutritious breakfast, snack, or dessert—Mediterranean Overnight Oats with Apricots and Pistachios! Store any leftovers in the refrigerator for up to 5 days.

Chapter 3: Appetizers and Snacks

Hummus and Veggie Sticks

Time: 20 minutes	Serving Size: 4 servings
Prep Time: 15 minutes	Cook Time: 5 minutes

Nutritional Facts Per Serving (1 serving):

Calories: 158, Fat: 8g, Total Carbohydrate: 16g, Protein: 6g, Sodium: 215mg.

Ingredients:

- 1 can of chickpeas, drained and rinsed, weighing 15 ounces total
- 1/4 cup tahini
- 2 tablespoons lemon juice
- 2 cloves garlic, minced
- 1/2 teaspoon ground cumin
- 1/4 teaspoon salt
- 2 tablespoons extra virgin olive oil
- 2-3 tablespoons water, as needed
- Paprika and chopped parsley for garnish (optional)
- Assorted fresh vegetables, such as carrot sticks, cucumber slices, bell pepper strips, and cherry tomatoes

Directions:

1. In a food processor, combine the drained chickpeas, ground cumin, minced garlic, lemon juice, tahini, and salt. Mix until thoroughly combined and smooth.

2. You have to process the hummus until it becomes smooth and creamy. Drizzle as much extra virgin olive oil as you can while the food processor is operating. One tablespoon of water can be added to the hummus to adjust the consistency if it's too thick.

3. You should taste the hummus to determine your own liking and modify the seasoning with extra cumin, lemon juice, or salt if needed.

4. When ready to serve, place the hummus in a bowl and garnish with chopped parsley and a pinch of paprika.

5. To make a vibrant and healthful snack tray, arrange the various fresh veggies around the hummus.

6. Your hummus and veggie sticks make a tasty and nutritious snack that is perfect for sharing with close friends and family. If you have any extra hummus, refrigerate it in an airtight jar for up to five days.

Tzatziki Dip

Time: 10 minutes	Serving Size: 6 servings
Prep Time: 10 minutes	Cook Time: 0 minutes

Nutritional Facts Per Serving (1 serving):

Calories: 60, Fat: 3g, Total Carbohydrate: 4g, Protein: 4g, Sodium: 150mg.

Ingredients:

- 1 medium cucumber, peeled, seeded, and grated
- 1 1/2 cups plain Greek yogurt
- 2 cloves garlic, minced
- 1 tablespoon fresh dill, chopped
- 1 tablespoon fresh mint, chopped (optional)
- 1 tablespoon lemon juice
- 1 tablespoon extra virgin olive oil
- 1/4 teaspoon salt
- 1/4 teaspoon black pepper
- Assorted fresh vegetables, pita bread, or pita chips for serving

Directions:

1. Once the cucumber is chopped to your desired consistency, wring out as much moisture as possible using paper towels or a dry dish towel. This is what prevents the dip from getting overly diluted.
2. Toss together the grated cucumber, Greek yogurt, lemon juice, extra virgin olive oil, minced garlic, chopped dill, chopped mint (if used), black pepper, and salt in a medium-sized mixing bowl. Mix the mixture thoroughly to make sure all of the ingredients are integrated.
3. When you sample the dip, adjust the seasoning with a little more salt, pepper, or lemon juice.
4. To let the flavors meld, cover the bowl and refrigerate for a minimum of thirty minutes. Although optional, this step improves the flavor of the dip.
5. To make a light and healthy Mediterranean appetizer or snack, serve homemade Tzatziki Dip with pita bread, pita chips, or fresh veggies. Any extra dip can be refrigerated for up to three days in an airtight container.

Mediterranean Bruschetta

Time: 25 minutes	Serving Size: 6 servings
Prep Time: 15 minutes	Cook Time: 10 minutes

Nutritional Facts Per Serving (1 serving):

Calories: 160, Fat: 7g, Total Carbohydrate: 20g, Protein: 4g, Sodium: 250mg.

Ingredients:

- 1 baguette, sliced into 1/2-inch thick pieces
- 2 cups cherry tomatoes, halved or quartered
- 1/4 cup pitted and chopped kalamata olives
- 1/4 cup red onion, finely chopped
- 1/4 cup fresh basil, chopped
- 1 clove garlic, minced
- 2 tablespoons of extra virgin olive oil, plus more for brushing the bread
- 1 tablespoon balsamic vinegar
- 1/4 teaspoon salt
- 1/4 teaspoon black pepper
- Optional: crumbled feta cheese for topping

Directions:

1. Turn the oven on to 375°F, or 190°C.
2. Gently brush each baguette slice with olive oil once you've placed them on the baking pan. Preheat the oven to a specific temperature. Toast the bread for 8 to 10 minutes or until

golden brown and crunchy. You should allow the bread to cool after removing it from the oven.

3. In a large bowl, combine cherry tomatoes, kalamata olives, red onion, basil, minced garlic cloves, 2 tablespoons extra virgin olive oil, balsamic vinegar, salt, and black pepper. Stir everything well to ensure it's all incorporated.

4. To allow the flavors to mingle, let the tomato mixture sit at room temperature for approximately ten minutes.

5. Evenly distribute the tomato mixture on top of each slice of toast. For an extra flavorful layer, top each bruschetta with crumbled feta cheese, if preferred.

6. Serve your colorful and tasty Mediterranean Bruschetta as a snack or appetizer that you can enjoy with friends and family. For optimal flavor and texture, serve this tasty and fresh dish at room temperature.

Greek Salad Skewers

Nutritional Facts Per Serving (1 skewer):

Calories: 80, Fat: 6 g, Total Carbohydrate: 5 g, Protein: 2 g, Sodium: 120 mg.

Ingredients:

- 12 cherry tomatoes
- 12 Kalamata olives, pitted
- 1 cucumber, cut into 1-inch chunks
- 1 red onion, cut into 1-inch pieces
- 1 bell pepper, cut into 1-inch pieces, of any color
- 6 ounces of feta cheese, cut into 1-inch cubes
- 1/4 cup extra-virgin olive oil
- 2 tablespoons red wine vinegar
- 1 teaspoon dried oregano
- For taste, salt and freshly ground black pepper
- 12 wooden skewers soaked in water for 30 minutes

Directions:

1. Thread a cherry tomato, an olive, a chunk of cucumber, a piece of bell pepper, a bit of red onion, and a cube of feta cheese onto a soaked wooden skewer to assemble the skewers. To make twelve skewers, repeat the method.

2. In a small bowl, whisk together the extra-virgin olive oil, red wine vinegar, dried oregano, salt, and black pepper to make the dressing.

3. Place the assembled skewers on a plate for serving. Coat every component equally by drizzling the dressing over the skewers.

4. Serve right away, or cover and chill for two hours to allow flavors to meld.

Marinated Olives

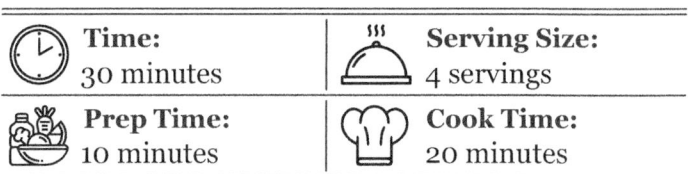

Nutritional Facts Per Serving (1/4 of the marinated olives):

Calories: 165, Fat: 16g, Total Carbohydrate: 4g, Protein: 1g, Sodium: 650mg.

Ingredients:

- 1 1/2 cups mixed olives (such as Kalamata, green, and black), pitted or unpitted
- 1/4 cup extra-virgin olive oil

- 2 cloves garlic, thinly sliced
- 1 tablespoon fresh lemon juice
- Zest of 1 lemon
- 1 teaspoon fresh rosemary, finely chopped
- 1 teaspoon fresh thyme, finely chopped
- 1/4 teaspoon red pepper flakes (optional)
- 1/4 teaspoon black pepper
- Fresh herbs for garnish (optional)

Directions:

1. Mix the mixed olives, extra-virgin olive oil, thinly sliced garlic, fresh lemon juice, lemon zest, chopped rosemary, chopped thyme, and black pepper in a medium-sized bowl. Make sure the marinade coats all of the olives by giving them a thorough stir.

2. Allow the flavors to fully meld together by marinating the olives for at least an hour, but overnight will yield the best results. Allow the olives to marinate in the refrigerator by covering the bowl with a cover or plastic wrap.

3. Take the marinated olives out of the refrigerator and let them sit at room temperature for ten to fifteen minutes before serving to allow the olive oil to resolve.

4. Move the olives to a serving bowl, pour over some of the leftover marinade, and top with fresh herbs, if preferred. As a tasty and nutritious Mediterranean snack or appetizer, savor your marinated olives.

Caponata Crostini

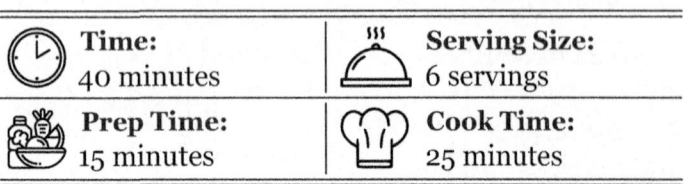

Time: 40 minutes	Serving Size: 6 servings
Prep Time: 15 minutes	Cook Time: 25 minutes

Nutritional Facts Per Serving (1 crostini):

Calories: 200, Fat: 8g, Total Carbohydrate: 24g, Protein: 7g, Sodium: 320mg.

Ingredients:

- 1 medium eggplant, cut into 1/2-inch cubes
- 1 red bell pepper, diced
- 1 medium onion, diced
- 2 cloves garlic, minced
- 1/4 cup Kalamata olives, pitted and chopped
- 2 tbsp capers, drained
- 1/4 cup pine nuts
- 1/4 cup raisins
- 1/4 cup fresh parsley, chopped
- 1/4 cup fresh basil, chopped
- 1 can (14.5 oz) diced tomatoes, drained
- 2 tablespoons red wine vinegar
- 2 tablespoon olive oil
- Salt and pepper to taste
- 1 baguette, sliced into 1/2-inch thick rounds
- Extra-virgin olive oil for brushing

Directions:

1. Warm the oven up to 400°F, or 200°C.

2. A large skillet is filled with two tablespoons of medium-high-temperature olive oil. Saute the eggplant, bell pepper, onion, and garlic for 10 minutes or until the vegetables are soft.

3. Add the diced tomatoes, raisins, parsley, olives, capers, and pine nuts to the pan. Simmer the mixture for a further 10 to 15 minutes, stirring frequently, until the desired consistency is reached. Incorporate the red wine vinegar and adjust the seasoning with salt and pepper to taste. After removing the pan from the heat, let it cool.

4. Lay the baguette slices out on a baking pan to bake while the caponata cooks. Drizzle each piece with extra virgin olive oil and toast for 6 to 8 minutes, until crisp and golden brown. Take the meal out of the oven and allow it to

cool.

5. Place a heaping dollop of the caponata mixture on top of each crostini before serving. Appreciate warm or room temperature.

Spinach and Feta Stuffed Mushrooms

Time: 30 minutes	Serving Size: 12 mushrooms
Prep Time: 10 minutes	Cook Time: 20 minutes

Nutrition Information:

Calories: 165, Fat: 11g, Total Carbohydrate: 10g, Protein: 7g, Sodium: 260mg.

Ingredients:

- 12 large white button mushrooms, stems removed and finely chopped
- 2 tablespoons olive oil
- 2 garlic cloves, minced
- 2 cups fresh spinach, chopped
- 1/2 cup feta cheese, crumbled
- 1/4 cup breadcrumbs (preferably whole wheat)
- 1/4 cup fresh parsley, chopped
- Salt and pepper, to taste
- 1 tablespoon lemon juice
- 2 tablespoons pine nuts (optional)

Directions:

1. Set oven temperature to 375°F, or 190°C.
2. A medium skillet should be filled with one tablespoon of hot olive oil. Once aromatic, sauté the garlic for about one minute after adding it.
3. Simmer for two to three minutes after adding the chopped mushroom stems to release any remaining liquid.
4. Incorporate the spinach when it has wilted.
5. After turning off the heat, give the mixture a little time to cool. Pour in the lemon juice, salt, pepper, breadcrumbs, feta crumbles, and half of the parsley. Combine thoroughly.
6. The filling should be pushed as firmly as possible within each mushroom cap after the spinach and feta mixture has been added.
7. Line a baking sheet with the stuffed mushrooms. Finally, drizzle in the remaining tablespoon of olive oil.
8. Bake, covered, until the mushrooms are tender and start to brown on top, for about 20 minutes.
9. Toast the pine nuts gently in a dry skillet over medium heat until they turn golden brown, stirring often, while the mushrooms bake. About three or four minutes will pass throughout this.
10. When the stuffed mushrooms are done baking, top them with the remaining parsley and, if desired, some brown pine nuts.
11. Serve it warm.

Falafel Bites

Time: 50 minutes	Serving Size: 4 servings
Prep Time: 20 minutes	Cook Time: 30 minutes

Nutrition Information:

Calories: 220, Fat: 10g, Total Carbohydrate: 27g, Protein: 7g, Sodium: 310mg.

Ingredients:

- 2 cups canned chickpeas, drained and rinsed
- 3 garlic cloves, minced
- 1 small onion, finely chopped
- 1/2 cup fresh parsley, chopped
- 1/2 cup fresh cilantro,

chopped
- 1 teaspoon ground cumin
- 1/2 teaspoon ground coriander
- 1/4 teaspoon chili powder
- 1 teaspoon baking powder
- 3 tablespoons all-purpose flour (or chickpea flour for gluten-free)
- Salt and pepper, to taste
- 4 tablespoons olive oil for frying
- Lemon wedges and tahini sauce, for serving

Directions:

1. In a food processor, blend the chickpeas, garlic, onion, parsley, cilantro, cumin, coriander, chili powder, baking soda, and flour. Process until smooth, but somewhat grainy. To taste, add salt and pepper.
2. Refrigerate the mixture for 15 minutes to solidify it.
3. Form the mixture into tiny, round bite-sized pieces, about one inch across.
4. Olive oil should be warmed in a large skillet over medium heat. The falafel bits should be added to the pan in batches while it's hot, being cautious not to pack it too full.
5. Fry for 4–5 minutes on each side, or until crispy and golden brown.
6. To drain excess oil, transfer the falafel bits to a plate covered with paper towels.
7. Serve hot with tahini sauce and lemon wedges.

Muhammara

Time: 35 minutes	Serving Size: 8 servings
Prep Time: 15 minutes	Cook Time: 20 minutes

Nutrition Information:

Calories: 160, Fat: 12g, Total Carbohydrate: 10g, Protein: 3g, Sodium: 75mg.

Ingredients:

- 3 large red bell peppers
- 1 cup walnuts, toasted
- 1/4 cup bread crumbs (whole wheat or gluten-free as desired)
- 2 garlic cloves
- 2 tablespoons pomegranate molasses (or lemon juice if unavailable)
- 2 tablespoons olive oil
- 1 teaspoon ground cumin
- 1/2 teaspoon red pepper flakes (adjust to taste)
- 1/2 teaspoon smoked paprika
- Salt, to taste
- 2 tablespoons chopped fresh parsley, for garnish
- Additional toasted walnuts, for garnish

Directions:

1. Bell peppers can be roasted by putting them directly over a gas flame or in an oven on broil. Turn from time to time so that the skin can blister and become black. After burning, place it in a bowl and cover it with a piece of plastic or cloth. Allow them to steam for ten minutes.
2. After removing the burnt peel and seeds, chop the roasted bell peppers.
3. Place the pomegranate molasses, roasted red peppers, toasted walnuts, bread crumbs, garlic, olive oil, cumin, red pepper flakes, smoked paprika, and salt in a food processor. Mix until well combined.
4. If needed, taste and adjust the seasonings.
5. Spoon into a serving bowl. As a garnish, sprinkle with a little toasted walnut, minced parsley, and olive oil.
6. Serve as a spread on toast or as an accompaniment to pita bread or fresh veggie sticks.

Chapter 4: Salads and Sides Dishes

Chickpea and Roasted Pepper Salad

Time: 25 minutes	Serving Size: 4 servings
Prep Time: 10 minutes	Cook Time: 15 minutes

Nutrition Information:

Calories: 280, Fat: 10g, Total Carbohydrate: 38g, Protein: 11g, Sodium: 290mg.

Ingredients:

- 2 cans (15 oz each) of chickpeas, drained and rinsed
- 2 large red bell peppers
- 1/4 cup fresh parsley, finely chopped
- 1 small red onion, thinly sliced
- 3 tablespoons extra virgin olive oil
- 1 tablespoon lemon juice
- 2 garlic cloves, minced
- Salt and pepper, to taste
- 1 teaspoon smoked paprika (optional for added flavor)
- Feta cheese crumbles (optional for garnish)

Directions:

1. The red bell peppers should be roasted first. Place them immediately on a gas burner or beneath the oven's grill. Occasionally turn, letting the skin sear and blister. Ten to fifteen minutes should pass.
2. When completely roasted, remove peppers to a bowl and cover. Let them steam for about five minutes. Because of this, peeling will be easier.
3. Once the peppers have steamed, remove the charred skin, discard the seeds and stems, and then chop the roasted peppers into small pieces.
4. In a large salad plate, add the chickpeas, diced roasted peppers, chopped parsley, and thinly sliced red onion.
5. In a separate small bowl, whisk together the olive oil, lemon juice, minced garlic, salt, pepper, and smoked paprika (if using) to make the dressing.
6. Blend the dressing into the chickpea mixture until well combined.
7. Taste and adjust seasoning. Before serving, top with crumbled feta cheese for taste.
8. You may serve it right away or refrigerate it for a few hours to allow the flavors to meld.

Mediterranean Beet Salad

⏰ Time: 45 minutes	🍽 Serving Size: 6 servings
🥗 Prep Time: 15 minutes	👨‍🍳 Cook Time: 30 minutes

Nutrition Information:

Calories: 215, Fat: 13g, Total Carbohydrate: 20g, Protein: 7g, Sodium: 120mg.

Ingredients:

- 4 medium-sized beets, peeled and diced
- 1 cup Greek yogurt
- 2 tablespoons fresh dill, finely chopped
- 1/4 cup walnuts, roughly chopped
- 2 tablespoons extra virgin olive oil
- 1 tablespoon lemon zest
- 2 garlic cloves, minced
- Salt and pepper, to taste
- 2 tablespoons crumbled feta cheese (optional for garnish)
- Fresh dill sprigs, for garnish

Directions:

1. Start the oven at 400°F (205°C).
2. Add the chopped beets to a baking dish, along with a tablespoon of olive oil, salt, and pepper. Please distribute them evenly across the surface in a single layer.
3. Bake the beets for approximately half an hour, tossing them halfway through, or until they are fork-tender.
4. Beets should be roasted while the dressing is being prepared. Toss together the Greek yogurt, chopped dill, lemon zest, minced garlic, remaining olive oil, salt, and pepper in a mixing bowl. Blend until well combined.
5. When the beets are slightly cool, add them to the yogurt mixture and toss again to coat well.
6. Salad should be moved to a serving bowl. Add some chopped walnuts, feta cheese crumbles, and fresh dill sprigs as garnish.
7. Before serving, chill for one hour to achieve a more blended flavor.

Fennel and Orange Salad

⏰ Time: 20 minutes	🍽 Serving Size: 4 servings
🥗 Prep Time: 15 minutes	👨‍🍳 Cook Time: 5 minutes

Nutrition Information:

Calories: 180, Fat: 12g, Total Carbohydrate: 18g, Protein: 2g, Sodium: 180mg.

Ingredients:

- 2 fresh fennel bulbs, thinly sliced
- 2 oranges, peeled and segmented
- 1/4 cup black olives, pitted and halved
- 1/4 cup fresh mint leaves, torn
- 3 tablespoons extra virgin olive oil
- 1 tablespoon red wine vinegar
- Salt and pepper, to taste
- 1 tablespoon fennel fronds (the green, dill-like tops of the fennel bulb) for garnish
- 2 tablespoons toasted almond slivers (optional for added texture)

Directions:

1. A mandoline or sharp knife should be used to thinly slice the fennel bulbs and arrange them on a platter.
2. Evenly scatter the orange segments over the fennel pieces.
3. Add a handful of chopped mint leaves and black olives to the salad.
4. Olive oil, red wine vinegar, salt, and pepper should all be combined in a small bowl and whisked to create the dressing.

5. Almonds and fennel should be covered equally with dressing.
6. Add toasted almond slivers and/or fennel fronds as garnish.
7. Serve it right away.

Tabbouleh

Time: 40 minutes	Serving Size: 6 servings
Prep Time: 15 minutes	Cook Time: 25 minutes

Nutrition Information:

Calories: 210, Fat: 10g, Total Carbohydrate: 27g, Protein: 4g, Sodium: 15mg.

Ingredients:

- 1 cup bulgur wheat
- 1 1/2 cups boiling water
- 2 cups fresh parsley, finely chopped
- 1 cup fresh mint, finely chopped
- 3 medium tomatoes, finely diced
- 1 cucumber, finely diced
- 3 green onions, thinly sliced
- 1/4 cup fresh lemon juice
- 1/3 cup extra virgin olive oil
- Salt and pepper, to taste

Directions:

1. Pour the boiling water over the bulgur wheat that has been placed in a large bowl. Once a plate or plastic wrap is placed over the bowl, allow the bulgur to soak for around thirty minutes, or until it has softened and absorbed most of the water.
2. Once the bulgur is cooked through, quickly toss it with a fork and let it cool to room temperature.
3. To the bulgur, add the chopped parsley, mint, tomatoes, cucumber, and green onions.
4. To make the dressing, combine the olive oil, salt, pepper, and freshly squeezed lemon juice in a separate, smaller bowl.
5. After adding the dressing to the bulgur and vegetable combination, toss until thoroughly combined.
6. To allow the flavors to mingle, refrigerate the tabbouleh for at least an hour before serving.
7. Serve chilled.

Roasted Red Pepper and Feta Spread

Time: 35 minutes	Serving Size: 8 servings
Prep Time: 10 minutes	Cook Time: 25 minutes

Nutrition Information:

Calories: 110, Fat: 9g, Total Carbohydrate: 4g, Protein: 3g, Sodium: 320mg.

Ingredients:

- 2 large red bell peppers (or 1 cup jarred roasted red peppers, drained)
- 1 cup crumbled feta cheese
- 2 garlic cloves, minced
- 2 tablespoons extra virgin olive oil, plus more for drizzling
- 1 tablespoon lemon juice
- 1/2 teaspoon smoked paprika (or regular paprika)
- Salt and pepper, to taste
- Fresh parsley, chopped (for garnish)

Directions:

1. Set the oven to 450°F (230°C) for self-roasted peppers. Spread out the bell peppers on a baking sheet and roast for about 30 minutes, flipping the peppers once or twice, until the skins brown. Take out of the oven and set

aside in a bowl. Cover with plastic wrap and let settle for approximately 10 minutes.

2. After the peppers have cooled, slice them, remove the seeds, and peel off the charred skins.

3. Place the roasted red peppers, crumbled feta cheese, minced garlic, olive oil, lemon juice, smoked paprika, salt, and pepper in a food processor. Blend until the mixture is smooth, but retains some texture.

4. If required, taste and adjust the seasonings.

5. Spread the mixture in a serving bowl, drizzle a little more olive oil over it, and cover it with chopped parsley.

6. Serve with pita chips, crusty bread, or sliced cucumbers.

Baba Ganoush

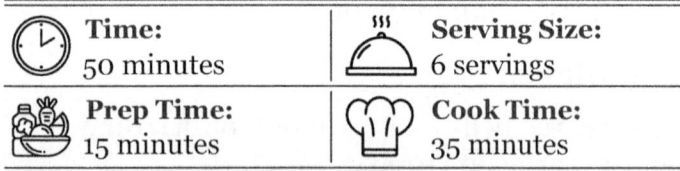

Time: 50 minutes	Serving Size: 6 servings
Prep Time: 15 minutes	Cook Time: 35 minutes

Nutrition Information:

Calories: 120, Fat: 9g, Total Carbohydrate: 10g, Protein: 3g, Sodium: 25mg.

Ingredients:

- 2 medium-sized eggplants
- 3 garlic cloves, minced
- 1/4 cup tahini (sesame seed paste)
- 3 tablespoons fresh lemon juice
- 2 tablespoons extra virgin olive oil, plus more for garnish
- 1/2 teaspoon ground cumin
- Salt and pepper, to taste
- Fresh parsley, finely chopped (for garnish)
- Paprika, for garnish
- 1 tablespoon sesame seeds (optional, for garnish)

Directions:

1. Set the oven temperature to 425°F (220°C).

2. To keep the eggplants from popping, prick them all over with a fork. Transfer them to an oven proof tray.

3. Bake the eggplants for about 40 minutes, or until the skin is browned and the insides are soft. To ensure even roasting, turn them occasionally.

4. When finished, take them out of the oven and let cool.

5. After the eggplants have cooled down sufficiently, remove the skin and transfer the flesh to a food processor.

6. To the food processor, add the minced garlic, tahini, lemon juice, olive oil, cumin, salt, and pepper.

7. The mixture should be smooth and creamy after blending.

8. Taste and adjust the seasonings as needed.

9. Transfer the baba ganoush on a dish for serving. Add a small amount of extra olive oil, sesame seeds, and chopped parsley and paprika, if desired.

10. Serve with pita bread or vegetable sticks.

Marinated Olives and Feta

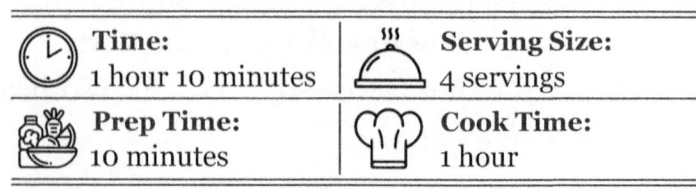

Time: 1 hour 10 minutes	Serving Size: 4 servings
Prep Time: 10 minutes	Cook Time: 1 hour

Nutrition Information:

Calories: 180, Fat: 16g, Total Carbohydrate: 4g, Protein: 5g, Sodium: 520mg.

Ingredients:

- 1 cup green olives (pitted)
- 1 cup black olives (pitted)
- 1 cup feta cheese, cubed
- 3 garlic cloves, thinly sliced
- Zest of 1 lemon
- Juice of 1 lemon
- 1/4 cup extra virgin olive oil
- 1 teaspoon dried oregano
- 1/2 teaspoon red pepper flakes (adjust to taste)
- 2 sprigs fresh rosemary
- 2 sprigs fresh thyme

Directions:

1. Place the black and green olives in a large mixing basin along with the cubes of feta cheese.
2. In a separate bowl, thoroughly combine together the chopped garlic, lemon zest, lemon juice, olive oil, dried oregano, and red pepper flakes.
3. Make sure everything is well coated by pouring the marinade over the olive and feta mixture.
4. Add the thyme and rosemary sprigs.
5. Gently toss to combine.
6. While the bowl is covered with plastic wrap, refrigerate. For the olives and feta, marinating for at least two hours is advised, but overnight is better for flavor.
7. Let it sit at room temperature for about 20 minutes before serving. Take off the thyme and rosemary sprigs.
8. Serve with crusty bread or as part of a Mediterranean antipasto platter.

Cucumber Yogurt Salad (Tzatziki)

Time: 1 hour 15 minutes	Serving Size: 6 servings
Prep Time: 15 minutes	Cook Time: 1 hour

Nutrition Information:

Calories: 80, Fat: 4g, Total Carbohydrate: 5g, Protein: 6g, Sodium: 25mg.

Ingredients:

- 2 cups Greek yogurt
- 1 large cucumber, peeled, deseeded, and finely grated
- 3 garlic cloves, minced
- 1 tablespoon fresh dill, finely chopped
- 1 table
- spoon fresh mint, finely chopped (optional)
- 2 tablespoons extra virgin olive oil
- 1 tablespoon fresh lemon juice
- Salt and pepper, to taste
- 1 teaspoon lemon zest (optional for added zestiness)
- Olive oil and a sprig of dill for garnish

Directions:

1. Grate the cucumber and place it in a sieve or strainer over a basin. When the salt has been added, let it sit for ten minutes.
2. Using your hands or a fresh cloth, squeeze as much water as possible out of the cucumber. By doing this, you can make sure your tzatziki doesn't become too thin.
3. In a bowl, combine squeezed cucumber, Greek yogurt, minced garlic, chopped dill, chopped mint (if using), olive oil, and lemon juice. Mix well and then stir in.
4. Add salt and pepper to taste. If you want a little more zing, add more lemon zest.
5. Before serving, cover and chill the mixture for at least one hour. This facilitates the blending of flavors.

CHAPTER 4: SALADS AND SIDES DISHES ◊ 33

6. Before serving, garnish with some dill and a drizzle of olive oil.

7. Serve cold as a light side salad, as a dip for pita bread, or with grilled meats.

6. Add some chopped cilantro or parsley and a squeeze of fresh lemon juice as garnish.

7. Serve immediately as a flavorful side dish to any main course.

Za'atar Roasted Carrots

⏰ Time: 45 minutes	🍽 Serving Size: 4 servings
🥗 Prep Time: 10 minutes	👨‍🍳 Cook Time: 35 minutes

Nutrition Information:

Calories: 120, Fat: 7g, Total Carbohydrate: 13g, Protein: 2g, Sodium: 80mg.

Ingredients:

- 8 medium-sized carrots, peeled and halved lengthwise
- 3 tablespoons extra virgin olive oil
- 2 tablespoons Za'atar spice blend
- 1 garlic clove, minced
- Salt and pepper, to taste
- Fresh parsley or cilantro, finely chopped (for garnish)
- A squeeze of fresh lemon juice

Directions:

1. Set the oven temperature to 425°F (220°C).

2. In a large mixing basin, thoroughly coat the sliced carrots with olive oil, Za'atar, chopped garlic, salt, and pepper.

3. Arrange the seasoned carrots so that they do not overlap when they are laid out on a baking sheet.

4. Bake for a quarter to a third of an hour, or until they are soft and nicely browned. Please turn them over quickly halfway through to ensure even roasting.

5. When finished, take the carrots out of the oven and place them on a platter for serving.

Lemon Herb Orzo Salad

⏰ Time: 25 minutes	🍽 Serving Size: 6 servings
🥗 Prep Time: 10 minutes	👨‍🍳 Cook Time: 15 minutes

Nutrition Information:

Calories: 220, Fat: 8g, Total Carbohydrate: 31g, Protein: 7g, Sodium: 180mg.

Ingredients:

- 1 1/2 cups orzo pasta, uncooked
- 3 tablespoons extra virgin olive oil
- Zest and juice of 1 lemon
- 1 cup cherry tomatoes, halved
- 1 cucumber, diced
- 1/4 cup fresh basil, chopped
- 1/4 cup fresh parsley, chopped
- 1/4 cup fresh mint, chopped
- 1/3 cup feta cheese, crumbled
- Salt and pepper, to taste
- Optional: 1/4 cup pitted Kalamata olives, halved

Directions:

1. Make sure to prepare al dente orzo pasta following the package's instructions. After giving it a good rinse in cold water, drain well.

2. In a large salad bowl, mix the lemon zest, juice, and olive oil. Season meal to taste with salt and pepper.

3. When the orzo has cooled, add it to the bowl and toss it with the dressing.

4. Incorporate the cherry tomatoes, cucumber,

optional olives, and fresh herbs into the bowl. Toss gently to mix.

5. Just before serving, add some crumbled feta cheese to the salad.

6. If needed, adjust the pepper and salt.

7. Serve chilled or at room temperature.

Chapter 5: Soups and Stew Recipes

Lentil and Spinach Soup

Time: 25 minutes	Serving Size: 4 servings
Prep Time: 10 minutes	Cook Time: 15 minutes

Nutrition Information:

Calories: 220, Fat: 5g, Total Carbohydrate: 32g, Protein: 12g, Sodium: 480mg.

Ingredients:

- 1 cup dried green lentils, rinsed and drained
- 1 large onion, finely chopped
- 2 garlic cloves, minced
- 1 carrot, diced
- 2 celery stalks, diced
- 4 cups vegetable broth or water
- 3 cups fresh spinach leaves, roughly chopped
- 2 tablespoons olive oil
- 1 teaspoon ground cumin
- 1 bay leaf
- Salt and pepper to taste
- Juice of half a lemon
- Fresh parsley, for garnish (optional)

Directions:

1. Heat the olive oil in a large saucepan over a medium flame. Add the celery, carrot, onion, and garlic to the pan and sauté until the vegetables are tender and translucent, about 5 minutes.
2. Stir in the bay leaf, cumin, and lentils. Toss the lentils in the oil and spices, and stir for one minute.
3. After adding the vegetable broth or water, raise the pot's temperature to a boil. Once the water reaches a certain point, reduce the heat to a low setting, cover the pool, and simmer the lentils for around 35 minutes, or until they are tender.
4. When the spinach has wilted, add it to the pot with the chopped spinach and simmer for a further five to seven minutes.
5. Add lemon juice, salt, and pepper for seasoning. Tailor the seasonings to your personal taste.
6. If preferred, top with fresh parsley while serving.

Chickpea and Rosemary Soup

Time: 1 hour 10 minutes	Serving Size: 6 servings
Prep Time: 15 minutes	Cook Time: 55 minutes

Nutrition Information:

Calories: 260, Fat: 7g, Total Carbohydrate: 40g,

Protein: 12g, Sodium: 550mg.

Ingredients:

- 2 cups dried chickpeas, soaked overnight and drained
- 1 large onion, finely chopped
- 2 garlic cloves, minced
- 1 carrot, diced
- 2 celery stalks, diced
- 6 cups vegetable broth
- 2 tablespoons olive oil
- 2 teaspoons fresh rosemary, finely chopped
- 1 bay leaf
- Salt and pepper to taste
- 1 tablespoon lemon juice
- Grated Parmesan cheese, for serving (optional)
- Additional rosemary sprigs for garnish (optional)

Directions:

1. A large saucepan is filled with heated olive oil at medium-low heat. Garlic, onion, carrot, and celery should then be added. Once the vegetables are soft, cook for a further five to seven minutes.
2. Fill the saucepan with the soaked chickpeas, bay leaf, and rosemary.
3. Bring to a boil after adding the vegetable broth.
4. Turn the heat down to a simmer, cover the pan, and cook the mixture until the chickpeas are fully cooked, about 1 hour after the mixture reaches a full rolling boil.
5. Do away with the bay leaf. Use an immersion blender to puree half of the soup, leaving some veggies and chickpeas whole, or gradually transfer to a stand blender.
6. Salt, pepper, and lemon juice are used to season the soup.
7. Serve hot with a dollop of Parmesan cheese and a rosemary sprig, if desired.

Tomato and Basil Soup

	Time: 45 minutes		Serving Size: 4 servings
	Prep Time: 15 minutes		Cook Time: 30 minutes

Nutrition Information:

Calories: 150, Fat: 10g, Total Carbohydrate: 14g, Protein: 3g, Sodium: 500mg.

Ingredients:

- 6 ripe tomatoes, roughly chopped
- 1 medium onion, finely diced
- 3 garlic cloves, minced
- 1/4 cup fresh basil leaves, chopped, plus additional for garnish
- 4 cups vegetable broth
- 2 tablespoons olive oil
- 1/2 cup heavy cream (optional for creaminess)
- Salt and pepper to taste
- 1 teaspoon sugar (optional, to reduce acidity)
- Freshly grated Parmesan cheese for serving (optional)

Directions:

1. A large saucepan is filled with heated olive oil at medium-low heat. Garlic, onion, carrot, and celery should then be added. Once the vegetables are soft, cook for a further five to seven minutes.
2. Fill the saucepan with the soaked chickpeas, bay leaf, and rosemary.
3. Bring to a boil after adding the vegetable broth.
4. Turn the heat down to a simmer, cover the pan, and cook the mixture until the chickpeas are fully cooked, about 1 hour after the mixture reaches a full rolling boil.
5. Do away with the bay leaf. Use an immersion blender to puree half of the soup, leaving some veggies and chickpeas whole, or

gradually transfer to a stand blender.

6. Salt, pepper, and lemon juice are used to season the soup.

7. Serve hot with a dollop of Parmesan cheese and a rosemary sprig, if desired.

8. Serve hot with a garnish of a few basil leaves and freshly grated Parmesan.

Mediterranean Fish Stew

Time: 1 hour 20 minutes	Serving Size: 4 servings
Prep Time: 20 minutes	Cook Time: 1 hour

Nutrition Information:

Calories: 295, Fat: 15g, Total Carbohydrate: 12g, Protein: 26g, Sodium: 550mg.

Ingredients:

- 1 lb white fish fillets (like cod, haddock, or halibut), cut into chunks
- 1/4 cup olive oil
- 1 large onion, finely chopped
- 3 garlic cloves, minced
- 1 bell pepper (any color), chopped
- 1 can (14 oz) diced tomatoes
- 1/2 cup white wine
- 1 cup vegetable or fish broth
- 1/2 cup kalamata olives, pitted and halved
- 1 teaspoon dried oregano
- 1/2 teaspoon dried thyme
- 1/4 teaspoon red pepper flakes (optional for added heat)
- Salt and pepper to taste
- Juice of 1 lemon
- 1/4 cup fresh parsley, chopped

Directions:

1. The olive oil needs to be warmed over medium heat in a big saucepan or Dutch oven. Add the garlic, onions, and bell pepper and sauté until transparent.

2. Add chopped tomatoes, white wine, broth, red pepper flakes, oregano, thyme, salt, and pepper. The blend is gradually simmered.

3. Before adding the fish chunks to the pot, ensure the broth has completely covered them. Fish should be cooked for 15 to 20 minutes, or until a fork comes out clean.

4. After adding the olives and lemon juice, simmer for five minutes.

5. Assess for seasoning, adding more or less salt and pepper as needed.

6. After removing the pan from the heat and adding the fresh parsley, serve hot.

Greek Lemon Chicken Soup (Avgolemono)

Time: 1 hour	Serving Size: 4 servings
Prep Time: 20 minutes	Cook Time: 40 minutes

Nutrition Information:

Calories: 210, Fat: 7g, Total Carbohydrate: 18g, Protein: 20g, Sodium: 580mg.

Ingredients:

- 4 cups chicken broth
- 1/2 cup uncooked orzo or rice
- 2 boneless, skinless chicken breasts, cooked and shredded (about 2 cups)
- 3 large eggs
- Juice of 2 large lemons
- Salt and pepper to taste
- 1 tablespoon olive oil
- 2 teaspoons finely grated lemon zest (for garnish)
- 2 tablespoons fresh parsley, chopped (for garnish)

Directions:

1. In a large pot, the chicken stock should be

heated to a boil. Add the orzo or rice and simmer until tender. If using orzo, cook, stirring occasionally, until rice is tender, about 20 minutes.

2. While the orzo cooks, beat the eggs in a separate bowl until frothy. Gradually whisk in the lemon juice.

3. Once the orzo is cooked, lower the heat. Gradually whisk in a cup of hot broth from the pot to the egg-lemon mixture, being careful to temper the eggs to prevent them from scrambling.

4. Return the egg-lemon mixture to the pot gradually while continuing to stir continuously.

5. Add the shredded chicken to the saucepan and slowly reheat it once the soup has slightly thickened and the chicken is cooked through. Boiling the soup could cause the eggs to curdle, so avoid doing that.

6. To taste, add salt and pepper for seasoning.

7. Serve the soup hot, drizzled with olive oil, and garnished with lemon zest and chopped parsley.

Turkish Red Lentil Soup

Time: 50 minutes	Serving Size: 4 servings
Prep Time: 10 minutes	Cook Time: 40 minutes

Nutrition Information:

Calories: 150, Fat: 2g, Total Carbohydrate: 24g, Protein: 9g, Sodium: 420mg.

Ingredients:

- 1 cup red lentils, rinsed and drained
- 1 large onion, finely chopped
- 1 carrot, peeled and diced
- 2 cloves garlic, minced
- 1 tablespoon tomato paste
- 1 teaspoon ground cumin
- 1/2 teaspoon smoked paprika
- 1/4 teaspoon ground turmeric
- 6 cups vegetable broth or water
- 1 tablespoon olive oil
- Salt and pepper to taste
- Juice of half a lemon
- Fresh mint leaves for garnish
- Red pepper flakes (optional, for added spice)

Directions:

1. In a large pot, olive oil is heated on medium-low heat. Diced onion should be added and cooked for 3 to 4 minutes, or until translucent.

2. Add the garlic and continue to sauté for one more minute when aromatic.

3. Stir in tomato paste, paprika, cumin, and turmeric. Cook for a further two to three minutes while stirring continuously.

4. Stir together the rinsed lentils and chopped carrot after adding them to the pot.

5. Bring the mixture to a boil after adding the water or vegetable broth. Reduce the heat to low and cover the saucepan to cook the lentils for 30 to 35 minutes, or until they are tender.

6. To achieve the required degree of pureeing, mix the soup using an immersion blender. Another option is to transfer the soup to a blender in batches. Just make sure that before blending, the soup has cooled down a bit.

7. If the soup was placed in a blender, then return it to the saucepan and add lemon juice, salt, and pepper to taste. To taste, adjust the seasonings.

8. Serve hot, topped with a few fresh mint leaves and, if you'd like some spice, some red pepper flakes.

Mediterranean Vegetable Soup

Time: 1 hour 15 minutes	Serving Size: 6 servings
Prep Time: 15 minutes	Cook Time: 1 hour

Nutrition Information:

Calories: 165, Fat: 4g, Total Carbohydrate: 27g, Protein: 6g, Sodium: 530mg.

Ingredients:

- 2 tablespoons olive oil
- 1 large onion, diced
- 3 cloves garlic, minced
- 1 zucchini, diced
- 1 red bell pepper, diced
- 1 cup cherry tomatoes, halved
- 1 cup green beans, chopped into 1-inch pieces
- 1/2 cup celery, diced
- 1 carrot, peeled and diced
- 6 cups vegetable broth
- 1 teaspoon dried oregano
- 1 teaspoon dried basil
- 1/2 teaspoon ground black pepper
- Salt, to taste
- 1 can (15 oz) cannellini beans, drained and rinsed
- 1/4 cup fresh parsley, chopped
- Juice of 1 lemon
- 1/2 cup small pasta (like orzo or ditalini), optional

Directions:

1. In a large pot, warm olive oil over medium-low heat. Add and sauté the onion until it becomes translucent.
2. Add the garlic and sauté for one more minute.
3. Add the carrot, celery, green beans, bell pepper, zucchini, and cherry tomatoes. When the vegetables soften, stir and simmer for about five minutes.
4. After adding the vegetable broth, bring the mixture to a boil.
5. Mix in the salt, black pepper, and dried herbs when boiling. Simmer the mixture over low heat.
6. Add the pasta to the saucepan now if using it.
7. Allow soup to boil for 15 to 20 minutes, or until vegetables and noodles (if using) are tender.
8. Add the cannellini beans and stir; allow to warm for about 5 minutes.
9. Take out the pot from the burner. Lemon juice and fresh parsley should be added. Mix well, adding seasoning if needed.
10. Serve hot, adding a drizzle of olive oil or some grated Parmesan cheese as a garnish.

Escarole and White Bean Soup

Time: 1 hour 10 minutes	Serving Size: 6 servings
Prep Time: 20 minutes	Cook Time: 50 minutes

Nutrition Information:

Calories: 215, Fat: 5g, Total Carbohydrate: 32g, Protein: 13g, Sodium: 680mg.

Ingredients:

- 2 tablespoons olive oil
- 1 large onion, diced
- 3 cloves garlic, minced
- 1 head of escarole, washed and chopped into bite-sized pieces
- 2 cans (15 oz each) white beans (such as cannellini or navy), drained and rinsed
- 6 cups chicken or vegetable broth
- 1 teaspoon dried thyme
- Salt and black pepper,

- to taste
- 1/2 teaspoon red pepper flakes (optional for added heat)
- Grated zest and juice of 1 lemon
- 1/4 cup freshly grated Parmesan cheese (for erving)

Directions:

1. In a large pot, the olive oil should be heated over medium heat. Add the diced onion and sauté it until it becomes translucent.
2. Saute the garlic for two more minutes after adding it.
3. Add the chopped escarole to the pot and stir occasionally until the escarole wits.
4. At this time, add the dried thyme, white beans, broth, salt, black pepper, and red pepper flakes (if using). Mix well.
5. The blend reaches a boiling point. Once boiling, reduce the heat to a simmer and let the mixture stew for around half an hour to allow the flavors to meld.
6. Add the lemon zest and juice to the soup and stir thoroughly just before serving.
7. If needed, adjust the seasonings by tasting them.
8. Serve hot, garnished with freshly grated Parmesan cheese.

Cretan Tomato Soup with Orzo

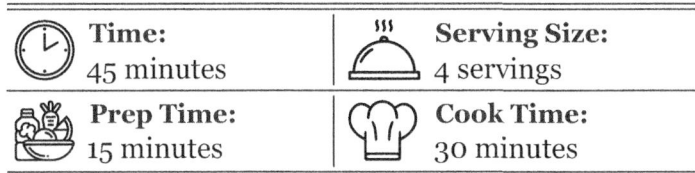

Time: 45 minutes	Serving Size: 4 servings
Prep Time: 15 minutes	Cook Time: 30 minutes

Nutrition Information:

Calories: 210, Fat: 7g, Total Carbohydrate: 32g, Protein: 6g, Sodium: 510mg.

Ingredients:

- 2 tablespoons extra virgin olive oil
- 1 large onion, finely diced
- 3 garlic cloves, minced
- 1 red bell pepper, diced
- 5 ripe tomatoes, diced or 1 can (28 ounces) diced tomatoes
- 6 cups vegetable broth
- 3/4 cup orzo pasta
- 1 teaspoon dried oregano
- 1/2 teaspoon dried thyme
- 1/4 teaspoon chili flakes (optional)
- Salt and black pepper, to taste
- 1/4 cup fresh basil, chopped
- Grated zest of 1 lemon
- Feta cheese crumbles, for garnish

Directions:

1. In a large saucepan, the olive oil should be heated over medium heat. When the onion is transparent, about 5 minutes after adding the diced onion, continue to sauté it.
2. Add the red bell pepper and garlic to the pot and sauté the mixture for an additional two to three minutes.
3. Add the orzo pasta, chopped tomatoes, veggie broth, thyme, oregano, chili flakes (if using), salt, and pepper. Heat the mixture until it boils.
4. When it reaches a boil, reduce the heat to a simmer, cover the pot, and cook the soup until the orzo is cooked through, 25 to 30 minutes at the most.
5. Add the lemon zest and fresh basil and stir.
6. Serve hot, garnished with a sprinkle of feta cheese crumbles.

Gazpacho

🕐	**Time:** 1 hour	🍽	**Serving Size:** 4 servings
🥗	**Prep Time:** 15 minutes	👨‍🍳	**Cook Time:** 45 minutes

Nutrition Information:

Calories: 135, Fat: 8g, Total Carbohydrate: 16g, Protein: 3g, Sodium: 420mg.

Ingredients:

- 6 ripe tomatoes, diced
- 1 cucumber, peeled, seeded, and diced
- 1 bell pepper, any color, seeded and diced
- 1 small red onion, chopped
- 3 cups tomato juice
- 1/4 cup red wine vinegar
- 1/4 cup extra virgin olive oil
- 2 cloves garlic, minced
- 1 teaspoon sugar
- Salt and pepper, to taste
- 1/2 teaspoon smoked paprika (optional)
- 1-2 slices of day-old bread, soaked in water and squeezed (optional for a thicker consistency)
- Fresh basil or parsley, for garnish

Directions:

1. Blend or process half of the tomatoes, cucumber, bell pepper, red onion, garlic, and bread (if using) until smooth.
2. Transfer the blend into a large basin.
3. To the blender, add the remaining tomatoes, cucumber, onion, and bell pepper. Pulse to chop finely, but do not puree.
4. Add the finely chopped vegetables to the bowl's pureed mixture.
5. Incorporate the tomato juice, red wine vinegar, sugar, olive oil, salt, pepper, and smoked paprika, if desired. Combine thoroughly by stirring.
6. As necessary, adjust the seasonings by tasting them.
7. To allow the flavors to meld, chill the gazpacho for at least two hours before serving.
8. Garnish with parsley or fresh basil and serve chilled.

Chapter 6: Pasta, Pizza, Rice, Pies Recipes

Pesto Fusilli with Cherry Tomatoes

Time: 30 minutes	Serving Size: 4 servings
Prep Time: 10 minutes	Cook Time: 20 minutes

Nutrition Information:

Calories: 450, Fat: 25g, Total Carbohydrate: 45g, Protein: 15g, Sodium: 320mg.

Ingredients:

- 2 cups fusilli pasta (whole wheat for a healthier option)
- 1 cup fresh basil leaves, packed
- 1/2 cup grated Parmesan cheese
- 1/3 cup extra-virgin olive oil
- 3 garlic cloves, minced
- 2 tablespoons pine nuts, toasted
- Salt and pepper, to taste
- 1 cup cherry tomatoes, halved
- 1/2 cup mozzarella pearls or diced mozzarella
- 2 tablespoons fresh lemon juice
- Zest of 1 lemon

Directions:

1. Heat a big saucepan of salted water to a boil. Al dente is the desired doneness, so add the fusilli pasta and cook as directed on the package. Remove and set aside.
2. Blend or food processor the basil, pine nuts, Parmesan cheese, and garlic until coarsely chopped; pulse.
3. Pour in the olive oil in a slow, steady stream while the processor is running. Stopping the processor to wipe the sides is necessary. Season to taste with salt and pepper.
4. In a large mixing bowl, mix together the cooked fusilli and the freshly made pesto. The pasta should be gently tossed until completely covered.
5. Add mozzarella pearls, lemon zest, lemon juice, and cherry tomatoes that have been cut in half. To ensure that every ingredient is evenly combined, toss again.
6. Serve immediately, garnishing with additional Parmesan cheese and basil leaves if desired.

Creamy Spinach and Mushroom Linguine

Time: 35 minutes	Serving Size: 4 servings
Prep Time: 10 minutes	Cook Time: 25 minutes

Nutrition Information:

Calories: 390, Fat: 12g, Total Carbohydrate: 55g, Protein: 17g, Sodium: 280mg.

Ingredients:

- 250g linguine
- 1 tablespoon olive oil
- 1 onion, finely diced
- 2 garlic cloves, minced
- 200g button mushrooms, sliced
- 100g baby spinach leaves
- 1/2 cup low-fat cream or Greek yogurt
- 1/4 cup grated Parmesan cheese
- 1/4 teaspoon red pepper flakes (optional)
- Salt and pepper, to taste
- Fresh parsley, chopped for garnish
- Zest of 1 lemon

Directions:

1. Follow the instructions on the package to make the linguine al dente. Once the linguine has been drained, reserve 1/2 cup of the pasta water in a cup. Set apart.
2. Fill a large pan with olive oil and turn the heat to medium. After sautéing, the onions become translucent.
3. Once again, sauté the minced garlic for one more minute until aromatic.
4. Once the fluids are released and the mushrooms start to brown, add the sliced mushrooms to the pan and simmer for 7 to 8 minutes.
5. Add the baby spinach leaves and simmer until wilted, about 1 minute.
6. After lowering the heat to low, pour in the cream or Greek yogurt and continue to stir until the mixture gets creamy.
7. After adding the grated Parmesan cheese, season with salt, pepper, and red pepper flakes if you prefer.
8. After adding the creamy spinach and mushroom sauce to the skillet, toss in the cooked linguine. If the sauce is too thick, add more pasta water to get the desired consistency and put aside.
9. Serve the linguine in bowls, garnished with fresh parsley and lemon zest.

Tomato and Mozzarella Farfalle

Time: 25 minutes	Serving Size: 4 servings
Prep Time: 10 minutes	Cook Time: 15 minutes

Nutrition Information:

Calories: 410, Fat: 18g, Total Carbohydrate: 47g, Protein: 19g, Sodium: 340mg.

Ingredients:

- 250g farfalle (bow-tie) pasta
- 2 tablespoons olive oil
- 2 garlic cloves, minced
- 1/2 red onion, finely chopped
- 400g cherry tomatoes, halved
- 200g fresh mozzarella cheese, cubed
- 1/4 cup fresh basil leaves, torn
- 1/4 cup grated Parmesan cheese
- Salt and pepper, to taste
- 1 teaspoon dried oregano
- 1/4 teaspoon chili flakes (optional)
- Zest of 1 lemon

Directions:

1. To make farfalle al dente, follow the instructions on the package. Retain 1/4 cup of the pasta water after draining the farfalle. Set aside.
2. Fill a large pan with olive oil and place over medium heat. Saute the red onion and garlic until they become transparent and fragrant, respectively.
3. Stir the cherry tomatoes and let them soften

for five to seven minutes.

4. Stir thoroughly after adding the dried oregano and, if using, the chili flakes to the pan.
5. Add the fresh mozzarella cubes to the sauce and stir, letting them melt a little.
6. Cooked farfalle should be added to the pan and thoroughly mixed to coat the pasta in the sauce. Use the pasta water that was set aside to thin the sauce if it seems too thick.
7. Add lemon zest and salt and pepper for seasoning.
8. Pasta should be served in bowls, with grated Parmesan cheese and torn basil leaves as garnishes.

Margherita Flatbread Pizza

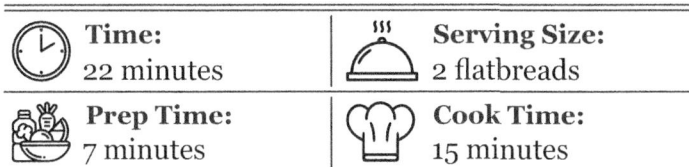

Time: 22 minutes	Serving Size: 2 flatbreads
Prep Time: 7 minutes	Cook Time: 15 minutes

Nutrition Information:

Calories: 460, Fat: 21g, Total Carbohydrate: 49g, Protein: 20g, Sodium: 680mg.

Ingredients:

- 2 large flatbreads or naan breads
- 1/2 cup tomato sauce (preferably homemade or low sodium)
- 1 cup fresh mozzarella cheese, thinly sliced
- 1 cup fresh basil leaves
- 1/2 cup cherry tomatoes, halved
- 1 tablespoon olive oil
- 1 garlic clove, minced
- Salt and pepper, to taste
- 1 teaspoon dried oregano
- Red pepper flakes (optional, for added spice)
- Freshly grated Parmesan cheese, for garnish

Directions:

1. Set the oven temperature to 425°F (220°C). If you're using a pizza stone, place it in the oven while it's heating up.
2. Spread your flatbreads out on a clean surface. Distribute the tomato sauce evenly over each flatbread.
3. Top the tomato sauce with the mozzarella cheese slices.
4. Distribute the cherry tomatoes, cut in half, across the cheese.
5. In a small basin, mix minced garlic with olive oil. Cover the tops of the flatbreads with this mixture.
6. Add salt, pepper, dried oregano, and red pepper flakes for seasoning, if preferred.
7. Place the cooked flatbreads in the oven (or, if using, directly onto the pizza stone). Bake for 12 to 15 minutes, or until the cheese is bubbling and starting to brown and the flatbread's edges are golden.
8. When the pizzas are done, top them with freshly cut basil leaves. As a garnish, add freshly grated Parmesan cheese.
9. Slice and serve immediately.

Mediterranean Veggie Pizza

Time: 30 minutes	Serving Size: 4 servings
Prep Time: 10 minutes	Cook Time: 20 minutes

Nutrition Information:

Calories: 480, Fat: 22g, Total Carbohydrate: 55g, Protein: 19g, Sodium: 820mg.

Ingredients:

- 1 pizza dough (store-bought or homemade)
- 1/2 cup tomato sauce (preferably homemade or low sodium)
- 1 cup fresh mozzarella cheese, thinly sliced
- 1/2 cup Kalamata olives, pitted and sliced
- 1/2 cup cherry tomatoes, halved
- 1/2 cup bell peppers (red, yellow, or green), thinly sliced
- 1/4 cup red onion, thinly sliced
- 1/4 cup artichoke hearts, chopped
- 1/4 cup feta cheese, crumbled
- 2 tablespoons olive oil
- 1 teaspoon dried oregano
- 1/2 teaspoon dried basil
- Salt and pepper, to taste
- Fresh basil leaves, for garnish

Directions:

1. Once the pizzas are out of the oven, sprinkle fresh basil leaves over them. As a garnish, sprinkle in some freshly grated Parmesan.
2. Roll out the pizza dough on a board dusted with flour to get the necessary thickness.
3. Place the dough that has been rolled out onto an inverted baking sheet or a pizza peel.
4. When distributing the tomato sauce evenly, the pizza crust should have a narrow border around the edges.
5. Lay slices of mozzarella on top of the sauce.
6. Add bell peppers, red onions, artichoke hearts, cherry tomatoes, and Kalamata olives on top.
7. Chopped feta cheese should be added to the top.
8. Mix the dried oregano, dry basil, salt, and pepper into the toppings, then dress them with olive oil.
9. Pizza can be baked in the oven on a baking sheet or carefully slid onto a warming pizza stone.
10. After the cheese starts to bubble and turn golden, and the crust turns golden, bake it for 18 to 20 minutes.
11. Take out of the oven and allow the dish to cool slightly before garnishing it with fresh basil leaves.
12. Slice and serve immediately.

Chicken and Pesto Pizza

Time: 30 minutes	Serving Size: 4 servings
Prep Time: 10 minutes	Cook Time: 20 minutes

Nutrition Information:

Calories: 540, Fat: 28g, Total Carbohydrate: 47g, Protein: 25g, Sodium: 840mg.

Ingredients:

- 1 pizza dough (store-bought or homemade)
- 1/2 cup basil pesto (preferably homemade)
- 1 cup cooked chicken breast, thinly sliced
- 1 cup fresh mozzarella cheese, thinly sliced
- 1/2 cup cherry tomatoes, halved
- 1/4 cup Kalamata olives, pitted and sliced
- 1/4 cup red bell pepper, thinly sliced
- 1/4 cup red onion, thinly sliced
- 2 tablespoons olive oil
- 1/2 teaspoon dried oregano
- Salt and pepper, to taste
- Fresh basil leaves, for garnish

Directions:

1. Select 475°F (245°C) as the oven's temperature. If using a pizza stone, place it in the oven during the preheating process.
2. On a lightly floured surface, roll out the pizza dough to the required thickness.
3. Roll out the dough and place it on an inverted

baking sheet or a pizza peel.

4. Spread the basil pesto evenly over the pizza dough, leaving a thin border around the borders.
5. Top the pesto with pieces of mozzarella.
6. Scattered throughout the cheese are the cooked chicken slices.
7. Add the red bell pepper, red onion, cherry tomatoes, and Kalamata olives.
8. Season the dish with salt, pepper, and dried oregano after giving it a quick olive oil spray.
9. Carefully slide the pizza onto the heated pizza stone or place the baking sheet into the oven.
10. The cheese should be bubbling and starting to brown after 18 to 20 minutes of baking, and the crust should be golden.
11. After removing it from the oven, give it some time to cool. A beautiful garnish is fresh basil leaves.
12. Slice and enjoy!

Lemon and Herb Risotto

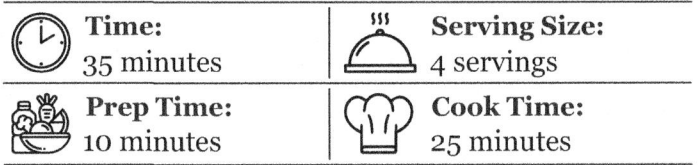

Nutrition Information:

Calories: 385, Fat: 12g, Total Carbohydrate: 56g, Protein: 10g, Sodium: 800mg.

Ingredients:

- 1 cup Arborio rice
- 4 cups vegetable broth
- 1 medium onion, finely chopped
- 2 tablespoons olive oil
- 1/2 cup white wine (optional)
- Zest and juice of 1 lemon
- 1/2 cup freshly grated Parmesan cheese
- 1/4 cup fresh parsley, finely chopped
- 2 tablespoons fresh basil, finely chopped
- 2 tablespoons fresh chives, finely chopped
- 1/2 teaspoon black pepper
- 1/4 teaspoon salt
- 1 tablespoon unsalted butter

Directions:

1. In a saucepan, reheat the vegetable broth over low heat.
2. In another large pan, melt the olive oil over medium heat. Add the onion and cook for four to five minutes, or until it becomes translucent.
3. The Arborio rice should be added and cooked, stirring regularly, for two to three minutes.
4. Add the white wine, if using, and stir until almost evaporated.
5. Stir constantly and add the warm vegetable broth half a cup at a time. Once almost all of the broth has been absorbed, stop adding more.
6. Continue cooking the rice according to these directions for at least 20 more minutes, or until it is creamy and al dente.
7. Add the lemon zest, juice, pepper, salt, chives, basil, and parmesan cheese. Simmer for two more minutes.
8. Turn off the heat and stir in the butter once it has melted and become smooth.
9. Serve immediately, garnished with additional herbs and Parmesan if desired.

Saffron and Vegetable Pilaf

⏰ Time: 50 minutes	🍽 Serving Size: 6 servings
🥗 Prep Time: 15 minutes	👨‍🍳 Cook Time: 35 minutes

Nutrition Information:

Calories: 265, Fat: 7g, Total Carbohydrate: 45g, Protein: 6g, Sodium: 480mg.

Ingredients:

- 1 cup long-grain rice (preferably Basmati)
- 2 cups vegetable broth
- A pinch of saffron threads
- 2 tablespoons olive oil
- 1 small red onion, finely chopped
- 2 cloves garlic, minced
- 1 cup diced bell peppers (red, yellow, and green)
- 1 cup zucchini, diced
- 1/2 cup peas, fresh or frozen
- 1/2 cup chopped tomatoes
- 1/4 cup chopped fresh cilantro
- 1/4 cup chopped fresh parsley
- Salt and freshly ground black pepper, to taste
- 1/2 teaspoon ground turmeric
- 1/4 cup toasted slivered almonds (optional)
- 1/2 lemon, juiced

Directions:

1. Till the water runs clear, give the rice a thorough wash in cold water.
2. Heat the veggie stock in a small saucepan. Five minutes after adding the saffron threads, let it soak.
3. In a large skillet or pot, reheat the olive oil over medium heat. Add the garlic and red onion and sauté until translucent.
4. Saute the zucchini and bell peppers for an additional five minutes, or until they soften.
5. Add the turmeric, tomatoes, and peas and stir. For seasoning, use freshly ground black pepper and salt.
6. Make sure all of the grains are covered with oil before adding the rinsed rice to the veggie combination.
7. Add the vegetable broth flavored with saffron and bring to a boil.
8. Reduce the heat to low, cover the pot, and simmer the rice for 20 to 25 minutes, or until it is tender and the liquid has been absorbed.
9. Take it off the heat and leave it covered for five minutes.
10. Fluff the pilaf with a fork, adding the fresh cilantro, parsley, toasted almonds, and lemon juice. Mix gently to combine.

Tomato and Olive Rice Salad

⏰ Time: 45 minutes	🍽 Serving Size: 6 servings
🥗 Prep Time: 15 minutes	👨‍🍳 Cook Time: 30 minutes

Nutrition Information:

Calories: 350, Fat: 12g, Total Carbohydrate: 52g, Protein: 8g, Sodium: 320mg.

Ingredients:

- 1 1/2 cups long-grain rice
- 3 cups water or vegetable broth
- 1 cup cherry tomatoes, halved
- 1/2 cup Kalamata olives, pitted and sliced
- 1/4 cup fresh parsley, finely chopped
- 1/4 cup fresh basil, thinly sliced
- 1 medium red onion, finely chopped
- 1 cucumber, diced
- 1/4 cup feta cheese, crumbled (optional for dairy-free diets)
- 3 tablespoons olive oil
- 2 tablespoons red wine vinegar
- 1 garlic clove, minced
- Salt and black pepper, to taste
- 1/2 teaspoon dried

oregano

Directions:

1. In a pot, first bring the water or vegetable broth to a boil. Once the rice has been added, reduce the heat to a low level, cover the pool, and simmer the rice for another 15 to 20 minutes, or until it becomes soft. Let the rice cool for a while.

2. In a large bowl, mix together the cooled rice, cherry tomatoes, olives, parsley, basil, red onion, and cucumber.

3. In another bowl, whisk together the olive oil, red wine vinegar, minced garlic, salt, pepper, and dried oregano. Drizzle the rice mixture with this dressing.

4. Toss the salad gently to make sure everything is evenly distributed.

5. If using, sprinkle crumbled feta cheese over the top.

6. To allow the flavors to meld, cover and refrigerate the mixture for at least an hour before serving. Kindly give it a quick swirl before serving.

Zucchini and Ricotta Galette

Time: 60 minutes	Serving Size: 6 servings
Prep Time: 20 minutes	Cook Time: 40 minutes

Nutrition Information:

Calories: 275, Fat: 17g, Total Carbohydrate: 23g, Protein: 10g, Sodium: 240mg.

Ingredients:

- 1 pie dough (store-bought or homemade)
- 2 medium zucchinis, thinly sliced
- 1 cup ricotta cheese
- 1/2 cup grated Parmesan cheese
- 1/4 cup shredded mozzarella cheese
- 1 garlic clove, minced
- 1 tablespoon olive oil
- 1 egg (for egg wash)
- 2 tablespoons fresh basil, chopped
- Salt and pepper, to taste
- 1/2 teaspoon lemon zest (optional)
- 1 tablespoon lemon juice

Directions:

1. Set oven temperature to 400°F, or 200°C.

2. On a surface dusted with flour, roll out the pie dough to a circular form 12 inches in diameter. Transfer to a baking sheet lined with paper.

3. In a mixing bowl, combine ricotta, Parmesan, mozzarella, zest from lemons, juice, and minced garlic; season with salt and pepper. Blend until thoroughly blended.

4. Leaving a 2-inch border around the edge, spread the ricotta mixture in the center of the rolled-out pie dough.

5. Lay the thinly sliced zucchini in an overlapping manner on top of the ricotta mixture.

6. To form a circle, fold the dough's edges over the filling, pleating them.

7. To give the galette a golden sheen when baked, brush the folded edges with a beaten egg.

8. Season the exposed zucchini slices with salt and pepper after drizzling them with olive oil.

9. Bake the galette for 35 to 40 minutes in a preheated oven or until the filling is bubbling and the crust is brown.

10. Remove from the oven and allow to cool for a bit. Before serving, garnish with fresh basil.

Chapter 7: Vegetables and Beans

Garlic Sautéed Green Beans

Time: 25 minutes	Serving Size: 4 servings
Prep Time: 10 minutes	Cook Time: 15 minutes

Nutrition Information:

Calories: 110, Fat: 7g, Total Carbohydrate: 11g, Protein: 3g, Sodium: 10mg.

Ingredients:

- 1 lb fresh green beans, trimmed
- 3 cloves garlic, minced
- 2 tbsp extra virgin olive oil
- Salt and pepper to taste
- Zest and juice of 1 lemon
- 1/4 cup sliced almonds (optional)
- 1/4 tsp red pepper flakes (optional for a bit of heat)
- Fresh parsley, chopped for garnish (optional)

Directions:

1. To retain green beans vibrant green but crisp, blanch them in a large saucepan of boiling salted water for two minutes. To stop the cooking process, drain the beans and set them in a basin of ice water. Drain again and set aside.
2. In a big skillet over medium heat, warm the olive oil. Add the minced garlic and sauté for an additional one to two minutes, or until the garlic starts to smell good but doesn't brown.
3. After turning the heat up to medium-high, add the green beans. After sautéing them for 5 to 7 minutes, stirring occasionally, they should be tender but still have a slight crunch.
4. Add the red pepper flakes and chopped almonds, if using, and sauté for a further two minutes.
5. Add salt, pepper, lemon zest, and lemon juice to the green beans. Mix thoroughly to blend.
6. Transfer to a serving plate and, if you like, garnish with fresh parsley. Serve instantly.

Chickpea and Spinach Stew

Time: 50 minutes	Serving Size: 4 servings
Prep Time: 10 minutes	Cook Time: 40 minutes

Nutrition Information:

Calories: 315, Fat: 10g, Total Carbohydrate: 45g, Protein: 14g, Sodium: 320mg.

Ingredients:

- 2 cans (15 oz each) chickpeas, drained and rinsed
- 1 large onion, finely chopped
- 3 cloves garlic, minced
- 1 tsp paprika (smoked or regular)
- 1/2 tsp ground cumin
- 1/4 tsp red pepper flakes (optional)
- 4 cups fresh spinach, washed and roughly chopped
- 3 tbsp extra virgin olive oil
- 1 can (14.5 oz) diced tomatoes
- 2 cups vegetable broth or water
- Salt and pepper to taste
- Zest and juice of 1 lemon
- Fresh parsley, chopped for garnish
- 1 tbsp tomato paste (optional for richer flavor)

Directions:

1. Warm the olive oil in a large pot or Dutch oven over medium heat. Add the onions when they become transparent, and cook for a further three to four minutes.
2. Add garlic, cumin, paprika, and red pepper flakes. Cook, stirring, for a further two minutes, or until aromatic.
3. Add the chickpeas and stir until the onion and spice mixture coats them thoroughly.
4. Add the water or vegetable broth, chopped tomatoes, and tomato paste (if using). After heating the mixture to a boil, the heat is reduced, and the mixture simmers for 20 minutes.
5. Stir in the chopped spinach and let it wilt in the broth.
6. Add lemon zest, lemon juice, salt, and pepper for seasoning. Simmer for a further five minutes.
7. Taste and adjust the seasoning if needed.
8. Serve hot, garnished with fresh parsley.

Eggplant and Bell Pepper Caponata

Time: 45 minutes	**Serving Size:** 6 servings
Prep Time: 15 minutes	**Cook Time:** 30 minutes

Nutrition Information:

Calories: 200, Fat: 11g, Total Carbohydrate: 24g, Protein: 4g, Sodium: 320mg.

Ingredients:

- 1 large eggplant, diced into 1/2-inch cubes
- 1 red bell pepper, diced
- 1 yellow bell pepper, diced
- 1 medium onion, finely chopped
- 3 cloves garlic, minced
- 2 tbsp capers, rinsed and drained
- 1/4 cup pitted and chopped green olives
- 1 can (14.5 oz) diced tomatoes
- 3 tbsp extra virgin olive oil
- 2 tbsp red wine vinegar
- 1 tsp sugar (or to taste)
- Salt and pepper to taste
- 1/4 cup fresh basil, chopped
- 1/4 cup fresh parsley, chopped

Directions:

1. In a big skillet, the olive oil needs to be heated over medium heat. Once the aubergine is chopped, add it and boil, stirring regularly, until it softens and browns, about 10 minutes.
2. Add the bell peppers, onion, and garlic. Sauté for 7 to 8 minutes, or until the veggies are tender.
3. Chop the tomatoes and add them with their liquids, then mix in the sugar, vinegar, capers, and olives. Add a little salt and pepper before serving.
4. The mixture should simmer for fifteen minutes when the heat is reduced to low. Take off the top and heat for 5 to 7 minutes to

give the flavors time to meld and the sauce a chance to thicken.

5. Remove from the fire and stir in the chopped basil and parsley.

6. Let the caponata cool a little. Warm or room-temperature serving options are available.

Lentil and Roasted Carrot Salad

Time: 40 minutes	Serving Size: 4 servings
Prep Time: 15 minutes	Cook Time: 25 minutes

Nutrition Information:

Calories: 320, Fat: 12g, Total Carbohydrate: 42g, Protein: 13g, Sodium: 280mg.

Ingredients:

- 1 cup dried green lentils, rinsed and drained
- 8 medium carrots, peeled and sliced diagonally into 1/2-inch pieces
- 3 tbsp extra virgin olive oil, divided
- Salt and pepper to taste
- 1/4 cup fresh parsley, finely chopped
- 1/4 cup feta cheese, crumbled
- 2 tbsp lemon juice
- 1 tbsp red wine vinegar
- 1 clove garlic, minced
- 1 tsp honey or maple syrup
- 1/4 tsp ground cumin

Directions:

1. Set the oven temperature to 425°F (220°C).

2. Add the carrots to a bowl and stir with one tablespoon of olive oil, a dash of salt, and pepper. Spread them out on a baking sheet and roast for 25 to 30 minutes, or until soft and lightly caramelized.

3. In a big saucepan, bring the water for the pasta to a boil while the carrots are roasting. Cook the lentils for a further 20 to 25 minutes, or until they are tender but not mushy, after adding them. After draining, set aside.

4. In a large bowl, stir together the cumin, honey or maple syrup, red wine vinegar, garlic, and the remaining olive oil. Salt and pepper should be added according to taste while seasoning.

5. While still heated, add the cooked lentils to the dressing. Toss in the coat.

6. After the carrots have finished roasting, let them cool for a short while. Add them to the lentils after that.

7. Gently whisk in the crumbled feta and chopped parsley after adding them to the salad.

8. Warm or room temperature salads can be served.

Mediterranean Cucumber and Tomato Salad

Time: 25 minutes	Serving Size: 4 servings
Prep Time: 15 minutes	Cook Time: 10 minutes

Nutrition Information:

Calories: 140, Fat: 10g, Total Carbohydrate: 11g, Protein: 3g, Sodium: 200mg.

Ingredients:

- 2 large cucumbers, peeled and diced
- 4 ripe tomatoes, diced
- 1/2 red onion, thinly sliced
- 1/4 cup kalamata olives, pitted and halved
- 1/4 cup feta cheese, crumbled
- 2 tbsp extra virgin olive oil
- 1 tbsp red wine

vinegar
- 1 tsp dried oregano
- 1 clove garlic, minced
- Salt and pepper to taste
- 2 tbsp fresh parsley, chopped
- 1 tbsp fresh mint, chopped (optional)

Directions:

1. In a big bowl, mix together the diced cucumbers, tomatoes, red onion, olives, and feta cheese.
2. In a separate small bowl, whisk together the olive oil, red wine vinegar, garlic, and oregano. Add salt and pepper to taste when dressing is prepared.
3. To coat all the ingredients and give the vegetable combination a little twist, drizzle the dressing over it.
4. If preferred, garnish with mint and fresh parsley.
5. To allow the flavors to mingle, let the salad sit for approximately ten minutes. Before serving, toss once more.
6. Serve chilled or at room temperature.

Stuffed Bell Peppers with Quinoa and Feta

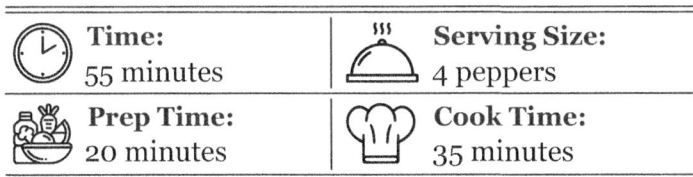

Time: 55 minutes	Serving Size: 4 peppers
Prep Time: 20 minutes	Cook Time: 35 minutes

Nutrition Information:

Calories: 310, Fat: 15g, Total Carbohydrate: 34g, Protein: 11g, Sodium: 550mg.

Ingredients:

- 4 large bell peppers (any color)
- 1 cup quinoa, rinsed and drained
- 2 cups vegetable broth or water
- 1 cup feta cheese, crumbled
- 1/2 cup cherry tomatoes, halved
- 1/4 cup red onion, finely chopped
- 2 cloves garlic, minced
- 1/4 cup fresh basil, chopped
- 2 tbsp extra virgin olive oil
- 1 tbsp lemon juice
- Salt and pepper to taste
- 1/4 cup pine nuts (optional)

Directions:

1. Set oven temperature to 375°F (190°C).
2. Extract the seeds and remove the tops of the bell peppers. Set apart.
3. In a saucepan, bring the vegetable broth or water to a rolling boil. Add the quinoa, cover the pot, lower the heat, and simmer until the liquid is completely absorbed, about fifteen minutes.
4. Toss the cooked quinoa with the feta crumbles, chopped cherry tomatoes, red onion, garlic, and fresh basil in a large bowl.
5. Drizzle the mixture with the extra virgin olive oil and a squeeze of lemon. Combine all the ingredients well, then season with salt and pepper.
6. Stir in the pine nuts slowly, if using.
7. Press down to push the food into each bell pepper after stuffing it with the quinoa and feta mixture.
8. Lay the stuffed peppers on a baking dish and tent them with foil.
9. Preheat the oven to 250°F. Cook for about 25 minutes. After 15 minutes, or until the peppers are fork-soft, remove the cover and continue baking.
10. Serve hot and enjoy!

Braised Cannellini Beans with Kale

⏱ **Time:** 1 hour 10 minutes	🍽 **Serving Size:** 4 servings
🥗 **Prep Time:** 15 minutes	👨‍🍳 **Cook Time:** 55 minutes

Nutrition Information:

Calories: 220, Fat: 7g, Total Carbohydrate: 30g, Protein: 10g, Sodium: 300mg.

Ingredients:

- 2 cups cannellini beans, soaked overnight and drained
- 4 cups kale, stems removed and roughly chopped
- 1 medium onion, finely chopped
- 3 cloves garlic, minced
- 2 tbsp extra virgin olive oil
- 1 tsp red pepper flakes (adjust to taste)
- 2 cups vegetable broth or water
- 1 bay leaf
- 1 tsp fresh rosemary, chopped
- Salt and pepper to taste
- Zest and juice of 1 lemon
- Grated Parmesan cheese for serving (optional)

Directions:

1. The best way to heat olive oil is to use a medium burner in a Dutch oven or other pot of comparable size.
2. Add the onions and cook for a further 3 to 4 minutes, or until they are transparent.
3. Saute the garlic and red pepper flakes for a further minute, or until aromatic.
4. Make sure the drained cannellini beans are thoroughly coated with the onion and garlic mixture by stirring them in.
5. Add the rosemary, bay leaf, and vegetable broth or water. Heat the mixture until it boils.
6. Once it reaches a boil, reduce the heat to low, cover, and simmer, stirring occasionally, for around half an hour.
7. 30 minutes later, add the chopped kale and stir. The kale should get tender after five to seven minutes.
8. Add salt, pepper, lemon zest, and lemon juice for seasoning. As necessary, adjust the seasoning.
9. Serve hot, optionally topped with grated Parmesan cheese.

Roasted Broccoli with Lemon and Garlic

⏱ **Time:** 30 minutes	🍽 **Serving Size:** 4 servings
🥗 **Prep Time:** 10 minutes	👨‍🍳 **Cook Time:** 20 minutes

Nutrition Information:

Calories: 115, Fat: 8g, Total Carbohydrate: 10g, Protein: 3g, Sodium: 40mg.

Ingredients:

- 4 cups of fresh broccoli florets
- 3 tbsp extra virgin olive oil
- 3 cloves garlic, minced
- Zest of 1 lemon
- 2 tbsp fresh lemon juice
- Salt and pepper to taste
- 1/4 tsp red pepper flakes (optional for added heat)
- 2 tbsp freshly grated Parmesan cheese (optional)

Directions:

1. Put some parchment paper or a silicone baking mat inside the oven and preheat it to 425°F (220°C).
2. Add the broccoli florets to a large dish and toss well with olive oil.

3. Add salt, pepper, lemon juice, zest, minced garlic, and red pepper flakes (if using). Till the broccoli is evenly seasoned, toss the combination.
4. Line the baking sheet with the broccoli and spread it out in a single layer.
5. The broccoli should be roasted for 15 to 20 minutes, or until it is soft and has some crunch on the edges.
6. If preferred, immediately grate some Parmesan cheese on top after taking it out of the oven.
7. Serve immediately as a side dish or enjoy on its own.

Zucchini Ribbons with Black Olives and Mint

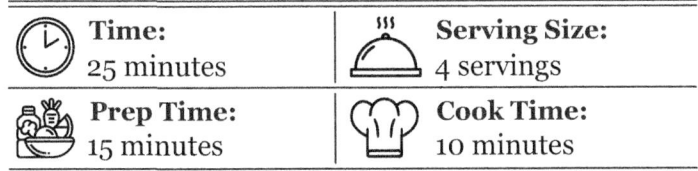

Time: 25 minutes	Serving Size: 4 servings
Prep Time: 15 minutes	Cook Time: 10 minutes

Nutrition Information:

Calories: 110, Fat: 7g, Total Carbohydrate: 8g, Protein: 3g, Sodium: 190mg.

Ingredients:

- 4 medium zucchinis
- 2 tbsp extra virgin olive oil
- 1/2 cup pitted black olives, chopped
- 1/4 cup fresh mint leaves, finely chopped
- 2 cloves garlic, minced
- Zest of 1 lemon
- 2 tbsp lemon juice
- Salt and pepper to taste
- 1/4 cup crumbled feta cheese (optional)
- Red pepper flakes (optional for added heat)

Directions:

1. Cut the zucchini lengthwise with a mandoline or vegetable peeler to create elegant ribbons. Distinguish.
2. In a large skillet, heat the olive oil over medium heat. Add the garlic once it becomes aromatic and boil it for about one minute.
3. Add the softened zucchini ribbons to the skillet and simmer for 3–4 minutes.
4. Incorporate the black olives, lemon zest, lemon juice, and half of the mint. Taste and add more salt, pepper, and red pepper flakes if desired. Cook for two to three minutes, or until the ingredients are cooked through and well combined.
5. Add the remaining mint and optional feta cheese crumbles to the serving platter after transferring.
6. Serve immediately as a side dish or light entrée.

Chard and Potato Gratin

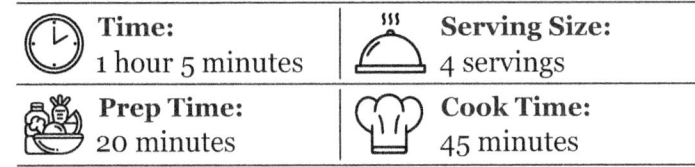

Time: 1 hour 5 minutes	Serving Size: 4 servings
Prep Time: 20 minutes	Cook Time: 45 minutes

Nutrition Information:

Calories: 420, Fat: 28g, Total Carbohydrate: 33g, Protein: 12g, Sodium: 340mg.

Ingredients:

- 2 lbs potatoes, thinly sliced
- 1 large bunch of chard (about 1 lb), stems removed, leaves chopped
- 2 cloves garlic, minced
- 2 cups heavy cream or half-and-half
- 1 cup grated Parmesan cheese
- 1/2 cup grated Gruyère cheese
- 2 tbsp extra virgin olive oil
- Salt and freshly ground black pepper, to

CHAPTER 7: VEGETABLES AND BEANS ◇ 55

- taste
- 1/4 tsp grated nutmeg
- 2 tbsp breadcrumbs

Directions:

1. Turn the oven on to 375°F (190°C).

2. In a large pot, the olive oil should be warmed over medium heat. Add the garlic and sauté until fragrant, about 1 minute.

3. Add the chopped chard and simmer for 4–5 minutes, or until wilted. Add nutmeg, salt, and pepper for seasoning. Take off the heat and place aside.

4. In another saucepan, reheat the heavy cream or half-and-half over low heat. Keep it from boiling. Add the Gruyère cheese and 3/4 of the Parmesan cheese, stirring until melted and mixed.

5. Before placing the chard mixture into a baking dish that has been prepared, place half of the potato slices in it. Pour half of the creamy cheese mixture over the chard.

6. Spoon the remaining cheese mixture over the potatoes that remain on top. Add the breadcrumbs and leftover Parmesan on top.

7. Bake for thirty minutes with the foil covered. Take off the lid and bake for 15 minutes, or until the potatoes are cooked through and the top is golden brown.

8. Before serving, give the dish a 10-minute rest period.

Chapter 8: Fish and Shellfish Recipes

Garlic Lemon Herb Grilled Salmon

- Time: 35 minutes
- Prep Time: 15 minutes
- Serving Size: 4 servings
- Cook Time: 20 minutes

Nutrition Information:

Calories: 310, Fat: 20g, Total Carbohydrate: 2g, Protein: 30g, Sodium: 85mg.

Ingredients:

- 4 salmon fillets (about 6 oz each)
- 4 garlic cloves, finely minced
- 2 tablespoons fresh lemon juice
- Zest of 1 lemon
- 3 tablespoons olive oil
- 1 tablespoon fresh chopped parsley
- 1 tablespoon fresh chopped dill
- 1 tablespoon fresh chopped basil
- Salt and freshly ground black pepper, to taste
- Lemon wedges, for serving

Directions:

1. Minced garlic, lemon juice, lemon zest, olive oil, parsley, dill, basil, salt, and black pepper should all be combined in a bowl. Blend thoroughly to form a marinade.
2. Place the salmon fillets in a shallow plate or a large, sealable plastic bag. Cover all of the salmon fillets with marinade by pouring it on. Once the bag or dish is sealed, place it in the refrigerator for at least half an hour.
3. Set the temperature of your grill to medium-high. Once the salmon is out of the marinade, allow any remaining liquid to run off.
4. Place the salmon on the grill and cook for about 6-7 minutes on each side or until it flakes easily with a fork and has light char marks.
5. Transfer the cooked salmon to serving platters, garnish with additional fresh herbs, if desired, and serve with lemon wedges.

Mediterranean Tuna Salad

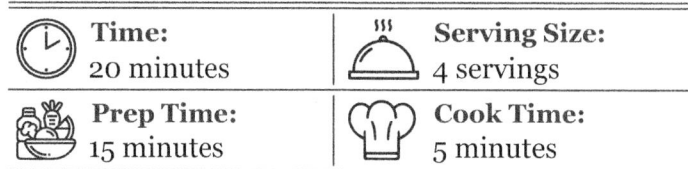

- Time: 20 minutes
- Prep Time: 15 minutes
- Serving Size: 4 servings
- Cook Time: 5 minutes

Nutrition Information:

Calories: 270, Fat: 16g, Total Carbohydrate: 8g, Protein: 23g, Sodium: 370mg.

Ingredients:

- 2 cans (5 oz each) tuna in olive oil, drained
- 1 cup cherry tomatoes, halved
- 1 medium cucumber,

diced
- 1/2 red bell pepper, diced
- 1/4 cup red onion, finely chopped
- 1/4 cup pitted Kalamata olives, halved
- 1/4 cup fresh parsley, chopped
- 2 tablespoons capers, drained
- 3 tablespoons extra virgin olive oil
- 2 tablespoons fresh lemon juice
- 1 teaspoon dried oregano
- Salt and freshly ground black pepper, to taste
- Optional: 1/4 cup crumbled feta cheese (omit for a dairy-free version)

Directions:

1. With a fork, crumble the drained tuna into a large mixing basin.
2. To the bowl, add the bell pepper, red onion, cucumber, cherry tomatoes, olives, parsley, and capers.
3. In a separate small dish, mix together the olive oil, lemon juice, dried oregano, salt, and black pepper to make the dressing.
4. After mixing the tuna and vegetables, drizzle the dressing over top. Mix everything together with a gentle toss.
5. For an extra flavorful layer, sprinkle some crumbled feta over the salad.
6. Serve right away or chill for an hour before serving to let the flavors meld.

Baked Tilapia with Tomatoes and Olives

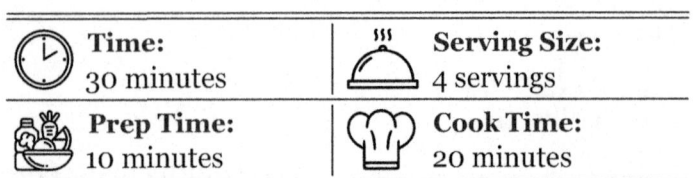

Nutrition Information:

Calories: 240, Fat: 12g, Total Carbohydrate: 6g, Protein: 28g, Sodium: 450mg.

Ingredients:

- 4 tilapia fillets (about 4-6 oz each)
- 2 cups cherry tomatoes, halved
- 1/2 cup Kalamata olives, pitted and halved
- 4 cloves garlic, minced
- 2 tablespoons extra virgin olive oil
- 1 tablespoon capers, drained
- Zest and juice from 1 lemon
- 1 teaspoon dried oregano
- 1/4 cup fresh parsley, chopped
- Salt and freshly ground black pepper, to taste
- Optional: crushed red pepper flakes for added heat

Directions:

1. Preheat the oven to 375°F (190°C).
2. Fill a large baking dish with about 1 tablespoon of olive oil.
3. Tilapia fillets should be arranged in the dish. Season each fillet with freshly ground black pepper and salt.
4. In a mixing dish, combine cherry tomatoes, garlic, olives, oil, capers, lemon zest, lemon juice, and dried oregano. Blend thoroughly.
5. Distribute the tomato and olive mixture over the tilapia fillets.
6. Not required:
7. For more spice, top with red pepper flakes.
8. Once the oven is ready, put the fish in and bake it for 20 to 25 minutes, or until a fork can easily pierce it.
9. Garnish with freshly chopped parsley before serving.

Easy Cod in Tomato Basil Sauce

Time: 25 minutes	Serving Size: 4 servings
Prep Time: 10 minutes	Cook Time: 15 minutes

Nutrition Information:

Calories: 230, Fat: 9g, Total Carbohydrate: 7g, Protein: 30g, Sodium: 360mg.

Ingredients:

- 4 cod fillets (about 4-6 oz each)
- 2 tablespoons extra virgin olive oil
- 1 medium onion, finely chopped
- 3 garlic cloves, minced
- 1 can (14 oz) diced tomatoes
- 1/4 cup fresh basil leaves, chopped
- 1/2 teaspoon dried oregano
- Salt and freshly ground black pepper, to taste
- 1/4 teaspoon red pepper flakes (optional)
- 1/4 cup freshly grated Parmesan cheese (optional for non-vegan)
- Fresh basil leaves for garnish

Directions:

1. In a big skillet over medium heat, warm the olive oil. Add the chopped onion and sauté for three to four minutes, or until it turns translucent.
2. Once aromatic, add the minced garlic and sauté for an additional minute.
3. Add the diced tomatoes with their juices. Add the dried oregano, chopped basil, salt, black pepper, and red pepper flakes (if using) and stir.
4. Simmer and boil the sauce for 8 to 10 minutes, stirring now and again.
5. After carefully tucking the cod fillets into the sauce, drizzle a little sauce over each fillet.
6. When the fish is well cooked and flakes apart easily when tested with a fork, add another 7 to 10 minutes of simmering time to the stew while keeping the skillet covered.
7. Before serving, sprinkle freshly grated Parmesan cheese on top if desired.
8. Garnish with fresh basil leaves before serving.

Mussels in White Wine and Garlic Sauce

Time: 40 minutes	Serving Size: 4 servings
Prep Time: 15 minutes	Cook Time: 25 minutes

Nutrition Information:

Calories: 225, Fat: 7g, Total Carbohydrate: 9g, Protein: 25g, Sodium: 570mg.

Ingredients:

- 2 lbs fresh mussels, cleaned and debearded
- 1 cup dry white wine (like Pinot Grigio or Sauvignon Blanc)
- 4 garlic cloves, minced
- 1 shallot, finely chopped
- 2 tablespoons extra virgin olive oil
- 1/4 cup fresh parsley, finely chopped
- 1 teaspoon red pepper flakes (optional)
- Zest and juice of 1 lemon
- Salt and freshly ground black pepper, to taste
- Crusty bread, for serving

Directions:

1. Heat the olive oil in a large saucepan or deep skillet over medium heat. Saute the chopped shallot until translucent, about 2 to 3 minutes.
2. Once aromatic, add the minced garlic and sauté for an additional one to two minutes.
3. After adding the white wine, squeeze in the

lemon juice and zest. Heat the mixture until it simmers gently.

4. Carefully add the cleaned mussels to the stew. Cook them covered for 5 to 7 minutes, or until they open up. Should a mussel not open, it should be thrown away.

5. Add salt, freshly ground black pepper, and red pepper flakes to taste.

6. Just before serving, stir in the freshly chopped parsley.

7. Serve hot with crusty bread to dip into the sauce on the side.

Olive and Caper Anchovy Pasta

Time: 25 minutes	Serving Size: 4 servings
Prep Time: 10 minutes	Cook Time: 15 minutes

Nutrition Information:

Calories: 380, Fat: 9g, Total Carbohydrate: 62g, Protein: 13g, Sodium: 680mg.

Ingredients:

- 12 oz spaghetti or linguine
- 2 tablespoons extra virgin olive oil
- 4-5 anchovy fillets, finely chopped
- 3 garlic cloves, minced
- 1/2 cup black olives, pitted and chopped
- 2 tablespoons capers, drained and roughly chopped
- 1/4 teaspoon red pepper flakes (optional for added heat)
- 1/4 cup fresh parsley, chopped
- Zest and juice of 1 lemon
- Freshly ground black pepper, to taste
- Grated Parmesan cheese, for garnish (optional)

Directions:

1. In a large saucepan, bring salted water to a rolling boil. When the pasta is al dente, add it and cook it according to the package's instructions. Save 1 cup of the cooking liquid after draining and putting the pasta aside.

2. In a large skillet, the olive oil should be warmed over medium heat. Add the anchovy fillets and heat, stirring constantly, for 2 to 3 minutes, or until they dissolve in the oil.

3. To make the minced garlic fragrant, sauté it for about a minute in the skillet.

4. Add the red pepper flakes, capers, and olives (if using). Allow the flavors to combine by cooking for a further two minutes.

5. Add the cooked pasta to the skillet and toss with the anchovies and olives. If the pasta seems too dry, add a small amount of the reserved pasta water to get the desired consistency.

6. Season with freshly ground black pepper and stir in the lemon juice, zest, and fresh parsley.

7. Serve warm, garnishing with grated Parmesan cheese if desired.

Baked Sardines with Lemon and Oregano

Time: 30 minutes	Serving Size: 12 sardines
Prep Time: 10 minutes	Cook Time: 20 minutes

Nutrition Information:

Calories: 230, Fat: 14g, Total Carbohydrate: 5g, Protein: 23g, Sodium: 290mg.

Ingredients:

- 12 fresh sardines, cleaned and gutted
- 2 lemons: 1 thinly sliced, 1 juiced

- 3 tablespoons extra virgin olive oil
- 2 tablespoons fresh oregano, finely chopped (or 1 tablespoon dried oregano)
- 3 garlic cloves, minced
- Sea salt and freshly ground black pepper, to taste
- 1/4 cup fresh parsley, chopped (for garnish)

Directions:

1. Set your oven's temperature to 375°F (190°C).
2. A mixing basin should be filled with olive oil, lemon juice, oregano, minced garlic, salt, and pepper. Mix well to combine flavors.
3. Sardines should be arranged in a single layer in a baking dish.
4. Make sure every sardine is well coated by pouring the olive oil mixture over it.
5. Put a piece of lemon between each sardine.
6. Bake for about 20 minutes, or until the sardines are cooked through and have taken on a hint of color.
7. Take them out of the oven after they're finished, and give them some time to rest.
8. Garnish with chopped parsley before serving.

Seared Scallops with Fennel Salad

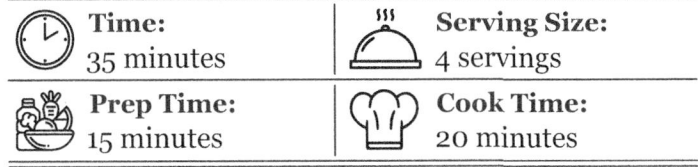

Time: 35 minutes	Serving Size: 4 servings
Prep Time: 15 minutes	Cook Time: 20 minutes

Nutrition Information:

Calories: 220, Fat: 12g, Total Carbohydrate: 15g, Protein: 15g, Sodium: 350mg.

Ingredients:

- 12 large sea scallops, cleaned and patted dry
- 1 large fennel bulb, thinly sliced
- 2 oranges, segmented
- 1/4 cup fresh mint, chopped
- 3 tablespoons extra virgin olive oil
- 1 tablespoon fresh lemon juice
- Sea salt and freshly ground black pepper, to taste
- 1 tablespoon unsalted butter (for searing)
- 1 teaspoon lemon zest, for garnish

Directions:

1. Combine the orange segments, mint, fennel pieces, two tablespoons olive oil, and lemon juice in a large mixing basin. When everything is thoroughly combined, toss gently and season with salt and pepper to suit. Put aside.
2. In a large skillet, cook the stick of butter and the remaining tablespoon of olive oil together over medium-high heat until the butter starts to foam.
3. Add a little salt and pepper to the scallops. Please don't pack them into the skillet too tightly.
4. Cook for 2 to 3 minutes on each side or until they have a beautiful brown crust. Take care to avoid overcooking.
5. Scallops should be taken out of the skillet and placed on a platter.
6. Arrange the fennel salad onto separate plates, including three scallops in each portion.
7. Garnish with lemon zest before serving.

Mediterranean Fish Stew with Potatoes and Olives

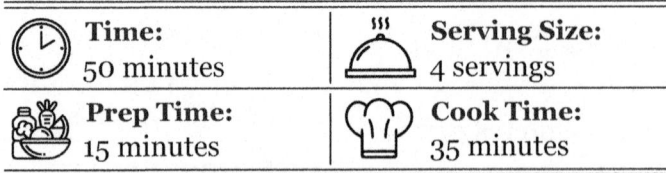

Nutrition Information:

Calories: 350, Fat: 10g, Total Carbohydrate: 30g, Protein: 30g, Sodium: 650mg.

Ingredients:

- 2 lbs white fish fillets (like cod or hake), cut into 2-inch chunks
- 3 medium potatoes, peeled and diced
- 1 large onion, finely chopped
- 4 cloves garlic, minced
- 1 cup green olives, pitted
- 1 can (14 oz.) diced tomatoes
- 1/2 cup white wine
- 2 cups vegetable or fish broth
- 1/4 cup fresh parsley, chopped
- 2 tablespoons extra virgin olive oil
- 1 teaspoon smoked paprika
- 1 bay leaf
- Salt and pepper, to taste
- Zest of 1 lemon

Directions:

1. You should preheat the olive oil in a big saucepan or Dutch oven. When the onions and garlic are translucent, add them and sauté for around 4–5 minutes.
2. Simmer for 5 minutes, stirring periodically, after adding the potatoes.
3. When it has reduced by half, around two to three minutes, pour in the white wine and simmer.
4. Season the pot with salt and pepper after adding the chopped tomatoes, broth, smoked paprika, and bay leaf.
5. Bring the mixture to a boil and simmer until the potatoes are almost done about 15 minutes.
6. Pour in the olives and the fish chunks. Until the fish is flaky and cooked through, boil it covered for a further 10 minutes.
7. Remove the bay leaf and stir in the fresh parsley and lemon zest.
8. Once you taste it, adjust the seasoning.
9. Serve hot in bowls, ensuring each serving gets a good amount of fish, potatoes, and olives.

Greek-style Shrimp Pasta

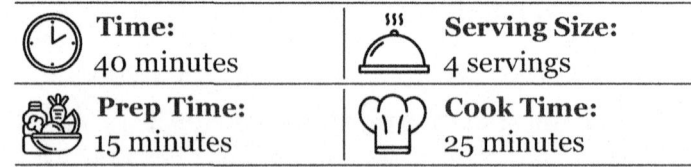

Nutrition Information:

Calories: 480, Fat: 18g, Total Carbohydrate: 52g, Protein: 28g, Sodium: 570mg.

Ingredients:

- 12 oz whole wheat spaghetti or linguine
- 1 lb large shrimp, peeled and deveined
- 3 cloves garlic, minced
- 1 medium red onion, thinly sliced
- 1 can (14 oz.) diced tomatoes, drained
- 1/2 cup Kalamata olives, pitted and halved
- 1/4 cup extra virgin olive oil
- 1/4 cup fresh basil, chopped
- 1/4 cup crumbled feta cheese
- 2 tablespoons fresh lemon juice
- 1 tablespoon dried oregano
- Salt and freshly ground black pepper, to taste
- 1/4 teaspoon crushed red pepper flakes (optional)

Directions:

1. Cook the pasta according to the package's

instructions in a large pot of boiling salted water until it's al dente. After draining, set apart.

2. Heat the olive oil in a big skillet over medium-high heat as the pasta cooks. After adding it for two or three minutes, the red onion should be transparent.

3. Stir in the garlic and sauté until fragrant, about 1 minute more.

4. Cook the prawns for 3–4 minutes, stirring occasionally, or until they turn pink on both sides.

5. Season with salt and pepper after adding the diced tomatoes, olives, oregano, and red pepper flakes (if using) to the skillet. To allow the flavors to mingle, simmer for 8 to 10 minutes.

6. Before adding the pasta to the skillet, ensure it is well combined and drains.

7. Fresh lemon juice should be drizzled on after adding crumbled feta cheese and chopped basil.

8. Serve immediately with additional feta on the side if desired.

Chapter 9: Poultry Recipes

Greek Lemon Chicken Soup (Avgolemono)

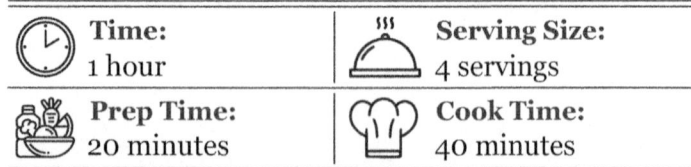

Time: 1 hour	Serving Size: 4 servings
Prep Time: 20 minutes	Cook Time: 40 minutes

Nutrition Information:

Calories: 210, Fat: 6g, Total Carbohydrate: 20g, Protein: 18g, Sodium: 880mg.

Ingredients:

- 4 cups chicken broth
- 2 boneless, skinless chicken breasts, cut into small pieces
- 1/2 cup long grain rice or orzo
- 3 large eggs
- Juice of 2 lemons
- 1 tablespoon olive oil
- 1 teaspoon salt (adjust to taste)
- 1/2 teaspoon freshly ground black pepper
- 1 tablespoon chopped fresh dill (optional for garnish)
- Lemon slices (for serving)

Directions:

1. In a large pot over medium-high heat, melt the olive oil. Add salt and pepper to taste along with the chicken bits. When the chicken is no longer pink in the middle, sauté it for four to five minutes.
2. Once the chicken broth has been added, the mixture will boil.
3. When it's boiling, add the rice or orzo. Simmer the rice and orzo for 20 minutes, or until soft, on medium-low heat.
4. In another bowl, whisk eggs and lemon juice together until frothy and smooth.
5. Stir the hot broth into the bowl with the eggs and lemon juice one ladleful at a time, whisking frequently to temper the eggs and prevent curdling.
6. Whisk continually as you slowly add the tempered egg-lemon mixture to the pot.
7. Cook, stirring frequently, over low heat for a further five to seven minutes, or until the soup slightly thickens. It shouldn't reheat to a boiling point.
8. If needed, taste and adjust the seasoning.
9. Serve the soup warm, garnished with fresh dill and lemon slices.

Chicken Kebabs with Tzatziki Sauce

⏰ Time: 45 minutes	🍽 Serving Size: 4 servings
🥗 Prep Time: 15 minutes	👨‍🍳 Cook Time: 30 minutes

Nutrition Information:

Calories: 270, Fat: 11g, Total Carbohydrate: 8g, Protein: 34g, Sodium: 320mg.

Ingredients:

For the Chicken Kebabs:

- 500g boneless, skinless chicken breasts, cut into 1-inch cubes
- 2 tablespoons olive oil
- 3 garlic cloves, minced
- Zest and juice of 1 lemon
- 1 teaspoon dried oregano
- 1/2 teaspoon ground cumin
- 1/2 teaspoon paprika
- Salt and freshly ground black pepper, to taste
- Wooden or metal skewers

For the Tzatziki Sauce:

- 1 cup Greek yogurt
- 1 small cucumber, finely grated and drained
- 2 garlic cloves, minced
- 1 tablespoon fresh dill, chopped
- 1 tablespoon fresh mint, chopped
- 1 tablespoon olive oil
- Juice of half a lemon
- Salt, to taste

Directions:

1. In a bowl, combine the olive oil, minced garlic, zest, and juice of the lemon, oregano, cumin, paprika, salt, and black pepper.
2. Ensure the chicken pieces are thoroughly covered with the marinade before adding them.
3. Give it a cover and chill for a minimum of half an hour.
4. Raise the temperature of the grill or grill pan to a comfortable level. To keep them from burning, soak wooden skewers in water for about twenty minutes.
5. The marinated chicken pieces are twisted onto the skewers.
6. After cooking for eight to ten minutes on each side, the chicken kebabs should be thoroughly cooked and golden brown.
7. To make the Tzatziki Sauce, mix together Greek yogurt, grated cucumber, garlic, dill, mint, lemon juice, olive oil, and salt in a basin. Blend until thoroughly blended.
8. Refrigerate the tzatziki sauce until it's time to serve.
9. Serve the chicken kebabs with the tzatziki sauce on the side.

Chicken Tagine with Apricots and Almonds

⏰ Time: 1 hour 30 minutes	🍽 Serving Size: 4 servings
🥗 Prep Time: 20 minutes	👨‍🍳 Cook Time: 1 hour 10 minutes

Nutrition Information:

Calories: 410, Fat: 24g, Total Carbohydrate: 30g, Protein: 25g, Sodium: 370mg.

Ingredients:

- 4 chicken thighs, bone-in and skin-on
- 1 large onion, finely chopped
- 3 garlic cloves, minced
- 2 tablespoons olive oil
- 1 teaspoon ground cumin
- 1 teaspoon ground coriander
- 1 teaspoon ground ginger
- 1/2 teaspoon ground cinnamon
- 1/4 teaspoon saffron threads (optional)
- 1 cup dried apricots, halved

- 1/2 cup blanched almonds
- 2 cups chicken stock or water
- Salt and freshly ground black pepper, to taste
- Fresh cilantro or parsley, for garnish
- 1 lemon, zested and juiced

Directions:

1. Over medium heat, warm the olive oil in a large tagine or other heavy-bottomed pot. The chicken thighs should be cooked for four to five minutes on each side after being placed skin-side down in the pan. Extract from the pot and set aside.
2. The same pot should be used to sauté the chopped onion until it becomes translucent. Add garlic, minced, and cook for an additional minute.
3. Season with the salt, pepper, cinnamon, ginger, coriander, and, if using, saffron. Make sure to thoroughly mix in the spices to coat the onions.
4. Along with the browned chicken thighs, add the almonds and dried apricots to the pot.
5. Once the chicken is halfway submerged, add the water or chicken stock. Heat to a rolling boil, lower the heat, place a lid on the pot, and simmer for around 60 minutes.
6. Verify and adjust the seasoning as needed. Add the juice and zest of the lemon and mix.
7. Add some fresh cilantro or parsley as a garnish right before serving.

Tuscan Chicken with Tomatoes and Spinach

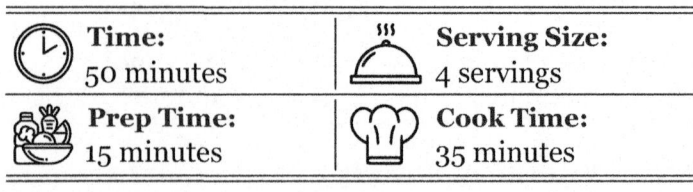

Time:	50 minutes	Serving Size:	4 servings
Prep Time:	15 minutes	Cook Time:	35 minutes

Nutrition Information:

Calories: 320, Fat: 18g, Total Carbohydrate: 8g, Protein: 31g, Sodium: 420mg.

Ingredients:

- 4 boneless, skinless chicken breasts
- 2 tablespoons olive oil
- 1 medium onion, diced
- 3 cloves garlic, minced
- 1 cup cherry tomatoes, halved
- 2 cups fresh spinach, roughly chopped
- 1/2 cup chicken broth
- 1/2 cup heavy cream or coconut milk (for a dairy-free option)
- 1/4 cup freshly grated Parmesan cheese (omit for dairy-free)
- 1 teaspoon dried basil
- 1 teaspoon dried oregano
- Salt and freshly ground black pepper, to taste
- 1/4 cup fresh basil, chopped (for garnish)

Directions:

1. On both sides of the chicken breasts, season with salt, pepper, dried basil, and oregano.
2. In a big skillet, the olive oil needs to be heated over medium heat. Add the chicken breasts and cook them until browned, about 7–9 minutes on each side. Once it has finished cooking, transfer it to a dish and reserve.
3. Transfer the chopped onion to the same skillet and cook over medium heat until it becomes transparent. Cook it for a minute more after adding the garlic.
4. Shake well to remove any browned parts from the bottom of the skillet before adding

the chicken broth. Give it a minute or two to simmer.

5. Add the cherry tomatoes to the pan and simmer until their skins start to split, about 4 to 5 minutes.

6. Reduce the heat to low and stir in the coconut milk or heavy cream, if using, and Parmesan cheese. Simmer the sauce for three to four minutes, or until it thickens.

7. The chopped spinach should be added to the hot skillet and stirred until it wilts.

8. Add the cooked chicken breasts to the skillet and let them simmer in the sauce for three to four minutes, or until they are heated through.

9. If required, taste and adjust the seasoning. Hot chicken should be served with fresh basil on top.

Spiced Chicken with Couscous Salad

Time: 60 minutes	Serving Size: 4 servings
Prep Time: 20 minutes	Cook Time: 40 minutes

Nutrition Information:

Calories: 360, Fat: 9g, Total Carbohydrate: 36g, Protein: 30g, Sodium: 310mg.

Ingredients:

- 4 boneless, skinless chicken breasts
- 1 tablespoon olive oil
- 1 teaspoon ground cumin
- 1 teaspoon ground coriander
- 1/2 teaspoon turmeric
- 1/2 teaspoon paprika
- Salt and freshly ground black pepper, to taste
- 1 cup couscous
- 1 1/4 cup boiling water
- 1/2 cup cherry tomatoes, halved
- 1/4 cup fresh parsley, chopped
- 1/4 cup fresh mint, chopped
- 1/2 cucumber, diced
- Juice of 1 lemon
- 1/4 cup crumbled feta cheese (optional)

Directions:

1. In a bowl, mix together the coriander, cumin, turmeric, salt, pepper, and paprika. Rub the spice mixture all over the chicken breasts, coating them completely.

2. Over medium heat, preheat the olive oil in a pan. Cook in the skillet for 6 to 7 minutes on each side or until the chicken breasts are done and golden brown. After removing the cooked meal from the heat source, set it aside.

3. Transfer the boiling water to a large bowl with the couscous. Cover with a lid or plastic wrap and let it lie for five minutes or until all of the water has been absorbed.

4. Flake the couscous with a fork and let it cool for a little while.

5. Toss in the crumbled feta cheese, cucumber, lemon juice, parsley, mint, and cherry tomatoes. Mix by tossing.

6. After cooking, slice the chicken breasts and serve them with couscous salad.

7. Optional: Drizzle with olive oil or a dollop of yogurt before serving.

Mediterranean Turkey Burgers

⏱ Time: 40 minutes	🍽 Serving Size: 4 servings
🥗 Prep Time: 15 minutes	👨‍🍳 Cook Time: 25 minutes

Nutrition Information:

Calories: 310, Fat: 15g, Total Carbohydrate: 16g, Protein: 28g, Sodium: 550mg.

Ingredients:

- 1 lb ground turkey
- 1/4 cup feta cheese, crumbled
- 1/4 cup black olives, chopped
- 2 tablespoons sun-dried tomatoes, finely chopped
- 1 clove garlic, minced
- 2 teaspoons fresh oregano, finely chopped (or 1 tsp dried oregano)
- 1 teaspoon fresh rosemary, finely chopped
- Salt and pepper, to taste
- 4 whole grain buns (optional)
- Toppings: lettuce, tomato, red onion, and tzatziki sauce

Directions:

1. In a big mixing basin, mix together ground turkey, feta cheese, black olives, sun-dried tomatoes, garlic, oregano, rosemary, salt, and pepper. Just whisk until mixed, being careful not to overwork the mixture.
2. Combine the ingredients in four equal portions; shape each into a patty.
3. A grill or grill pan needs to be at a medium temperature.
4. The turkey patties should be added to the hot pan and cooked for 6–7 minutes on each side, or until the internal temperature reaches 165°F (74°C) and the cakes are wonderfully browned).
5. For a couple of minutes, toast the buns, if using, under the grill until they start to become golden.
6. Burger assembly: After adding your preferred toppings, place a patty on the bottom half of each bun. Using the top bun half, generously coat the burger with tzatziki sauce.
7. Serve immediately with a side salad or your favorite Mediterranean side dish.

Chicken Shawarma Wraps

⏱ Time: 45 minutes	🍽 Serving Size: 4 servings
🥗 Prep Time: 15 minutes	👨‍🍳 Cook Time: 30 minutes

Nutrition Information:

Calories: 380, Fat: 12g, Total Carbohydrate: 35g, Protein: 32g, Sodium: 480mg.

Ingredients:

- 1 lb boneless, skinless chicken breasts or thighs, thinly sliced
- 4 whole grain or pita wraps
- 2 tablespoons olive oil
- 2 cloves garlic, minced
- 1 teaspoon ground cumin
- 1 teaspoon ground paprika
- 1/2 teaspoon turmeric
- 1/2 teaspoon ground coriander
- 1/4 teaspoon ground cinnamon
- Salt and pepper, to taste
- 1/2 cup plain Greek yogurt
- 1/4 cup cucumber, finely diced
- 1/4 cup fresh parsley, chopped
- Juice of 1 lemon
- Optional toppings: lettuce, tomato, onion, pickles

Directions:

1. In a mixing dish, whisk together olive oil, garlic, cumin, paprika, turmeric, coriander, cinnamon, salt, and pepper. Stir well.
2. Ensure all chicken slices are thoroughly

coated before adding them to the marinade. Give it ten minutes or so to marinade, but longer is preferable.

3. In a separate bowl, mix the Greek yogurt, cucumber, parsley, and lemon juice to make a simple tzatziki sauce. Season with a pinch of salt and set aside.

4. Heat a skillet or other pan over medium heat. The marinated chicken pieces should be added to the heated pan and cooked for 5 to 7 minutes on each side, or until the chicken is cooked through and lightly seared.

5. In a dry skillet, reheat the wraps for 30 seconds on each side.

6. To assemble the wraps, arrange the cooked chicken pieces on top of a teaspoon of tzatziki sauce. As desired, add the optional toppings.

7. Serve the wrap immediately after rolling it up and tucking the sides in.

Lemon Olive Chicken Thighs

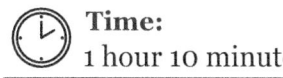 Time: 1 hour 10 minutes	Serving Size: 4 servings
 Prep Time: 20 minutes	Cook Time: 50 minutes

Nutrition Information:

Calories: 360, Fat: 28g, Total Carbohydrate: 4g, Protein: 23g, Sodium: 350mg.

Ingredients:

- 4 bone-in, skin-on chicken thighs
- 1/4 cup pitted Kalamata olives, halved
- 3 tablespoons extra virgin olive oil
- Zest and juice of 1 large lemon
- 4 garlic cloves, minced
- 2 teaspoons dried oregano
- 1 teaspoon dried rosemary
- 1/2 cup chicken broth
- Salt and pepper, to taste
- Fresh parsley, chopped for garnish

Directions:

1. Turn on the oven to 375°F (190°C).

2. Combine the lemon zest, lemon juice, garlic, oregano, rosemary, olive oil, salt, and pepper in a large bowl. After adding the marinade to the chicken thighs, toss to coat evenly.

3. Warm up a sizable oven-safe skillet over medium-high heat. Cook for approximately 4–5 minutes, or until the skin is golden brown, on the chicken thighs with the skin side down. After flipping, cook for a further 3 minutes.

4. After halving the Kalamata olives, distribute them among the chicken thighs in the skillet.

5. Drizzle the thighs with the chicken stock. This will help create a tasty base for a sauce and keep the chicken moist while it bakes.

6. Preheat the oven to 165 degrees Celsius (74 degrees Fahrenheit). Cook the chicken thighs in the skillet for 20 to 25 minutes, or until they are cooked through.

7. After removing from the oven, give it some time to rest. Before serving, sprinkle some fresh parsley on top.

Garlic Rosemary Roasted Chicken

Time: 1 hour 30 minutes	Serving Size: 4 servings
Prep Time: 20 minutes	Cook Time: 1 hour 10 minutes

Nutrition Information:

Calories: 460, Fat: 23g, Total Carbohydrate: 25g, Protein: 37g, Sodium: 420mg.

Ingredients:

- 1 whole chicken (about 3.5-4 pounds)
- 5 cloves garlic, minced
- 3 tablespoons fresh rosemary, chopped
- 3 tablespoons extra virgin olive oil
- Zest and juice of 1 lemon
- 1 teaspoon sea salt
- 1/2 teaspoon freshly ground black pepper
- 1/2 cup chicken broth
- 1 medium onion, cut into wedges
- 2 medium carrots, chopped into 2-inch pieces
- 8 small baby potatoes, halved

Directions:

1. Preheat your oven to 425°F (220°C).
2. After cleaning, use paper towels to dry the chicken. Eliminate giblets and excess fat.
3. Minced garlic, chopped rosemary, olive oil, lemon juice, lemon zest, salt, and pepper should all be combined in a small bowl to form a paste.
4. After gently removing the chicken breast's skin, coat the bird well with a rosemary-garlic paste massage.
5. After the lemon has been juiced, stuff the bird cavity with a few onion slices.
6. Spoon the remaining onion slices, then surround a roasting pan with the carrots and tiny potatoes. Add the chicken on top.
7. Fill the roasting pan with the chicken broth. In addition to keeping the veggies wet, this will provide a delicious base for gravy, should you choose.
8. Preheat the oven to 375°F (149°C). Roast the chicken for about 1 hour and ten minutes, or until the internal temperature reaches 165°F. Use aluminum foil to cover and bake the chicken if it's browning too soon.
9. Let the chicken rest for about 10 minutes before carving. Serve with the roasted vegetables.

Mediterranean Chicken Salad with Olives and Feta

Time: 25 minutes	Serving Size: 4 servings
Prep Time: 15 minutes	Cook Time: 10 minutes

Nutrition Information:

Calories: 290, Fat: 16g, Total Carbohydrate: 12g, Protein: 25g, Sodium: 480mg.

Ingredients:

- 2 boneless, skinless chicken breasts
- 2 tablespoons extra virgin olive oil
- 1 teaspoon dried oregano
- Salt and freshly ground black pepper, to taste
- 4 cups mixed salad greens (like spinach, arugula, and romaine)
- 1 cup cherry tomatoes, halved
- 1 cucumber, sliced
- 1/2 cup Kalamata olives, pitted and sliced
- 1/4 cup red onion, thinly sliced
- 1/2 cup crumbled feta cheese
- 3 tablespoons balsamic vinaigrette

Directions:

1. Add black pepper, salt, oregano, and olive oil to chicken breasts for seasoning. Make sure to coat both sides well.
2. Heat a grill or a skillet over a medium-high heat source to prepare it. When the chicken is fully cooked and the center is no longer pink, add the chicken breasts and sauté them for about 4–5 minutes on each side.
3. Once the chicken is done cooking, remove it from the flame and give it some time to rest.

Cut it into easily ingested pieces after that.

4. In a large salad bowl, mix together salad greens, cherry tomatoes, cucumber, Kalamata olives, and red onion.

5. Add the feta cheese crumbles, balsamic vinaigrette, and sliced chicken to the salad. Gently toss to mix in all the ingredients.

6. Immediately serve as a side dish with crusty bread or as a main course.

Chapter 10: Beef, Pork, Lamb Recipes

Grilled Lamb Chops with Mint Sauce

	Time: 60 minutes		Serving Size: 4 servings
	Prep Time: 20 minutes		Cook Time: 40 minutes

Nutrition Information:

Calories: 310, Fat: 21g, Total Carbohydrate: 5g, Protein: 24g, Sodium: 90mg.

Ingredients:

- 8 lamb chops
- 2 tablespoons extra virgin olive oil
- 2 garlic cloves, minced
- 1 teaspoon rosemary, finely chopped
- Salt and freshly ground black pepper, to taste
- Zest of 1 lemon
- For the Mint Sauce:
- 1 cup fresh mint leaves, finely chopped
- 1/4 cup boiling water
- 2 tablespoons white wine vinegar
- 1 tablespoon sugar
- Pinch of salt

Directions:

1. In a mixing dish, combine olive oil, minced garlic, chopped rosemary, lemon zest, and a dash of salt and black pepper. Mix well.
2. Make sure the lamb chops are evenly coated by brushing them with the mixture. Give them at least ten minutes to marinade.
3. Make the mint sauce while the lamb is marinating. The chopped mint should be put in a small basin. Over the mint, pour boiling water, and steep for approximately five minutes.
4. Empty the water and drain the mint when it has steeped.
5. Mix the mint with sugar, white wine vinegar, and a small amount of salt.
6. Stir thoroughly and reserve.
7. To prepare a skillet or grill for use:
8. Turn the heat up to a medium-high flame.
9. Once the lamb chops are on the grill, cook them for about 6–7 minutes on each side for medium-rare, or until they are done to your preference.
10. Once the lamb chops are done grilling, remove from the heat and set aside to rest for a few minutes.
11. Serve the grilled lamb chops with a generous drizzle of the prepared mint sauce.

Beef and Eggplant Moussaka

Time: 1 hour 45 minutes
Serving Size: 6 servings
Prep Time: 30 minutes
Cook Time: 1 hour 15 minutes

Nutrition Information:

Calories: 420, Fat: 28g, Total Carbohydrate: 25g, Protein: 18g, Sodium: 300mg.

Ingredients:

- 2 large eggplants, thinly sliced
- 1 lb ground beef
- 1 onion, finely chopped
- 2 garlic cloves, minced
- 1 can (14 oz) crushed tomatoes
- 2 tablespoons tomato paste
- 1/4 cup red wine
- 1 teaspoon ground cinnamon
- 1/2 teaspoon ground nutmeg
- 2 tablespoons fresh parsley, chopped
- Salt and pepper to taste
- 3 tablespoons olive oil
- For the Béchamel Sauce:
- 4 tablespoons unsalted butter
- 4 tablespoons all-purpose flour
- 2 cups milk
- 1/4 teaspoon grated nutmeg
- 1/2 cup grated Parmesan cheese
- Salt to taste
- 2 eggs, beaten

Directions:

1. Preheat your oven to 400°F (200°C).
2. Brush the baking sheet with a small amount of olive oil before adding the eggplant pieces. When the food is soft and browned, roast it for about 20 minutes, turning the pan halfway through, adding salt and pepper to taste.
3. Heat a skillet with olive oil and sauté the onions until they become translucent. Brown the ground meat by adding the garlic and sautéing it.
4. Add salt, pepper, cinnamon, nutmeg, red wine, smashed tomatoes, and tomato paste. After 15 to 20 minutes of simmering, set aside the mixture.
5. The butter should be melted in a pot for the béchamel sauce. Cook for a few minutes while stirring continuously after adding the flour. To avoid lumps, gradually add the milk while stirring constantly. Add nutmeg and salt for seasoning, and boil until the sauce thickens.
6. Put the beaten eggs and Parmesan cheese in after removing the heat source. Whisk quickly to avoid the heat scrambling the eggs.
7. Half of the roasted eggplant slices should be layered in a large baking dish. Over the eggplants, distribute the beef mixture. Top with the remaining slices of eggplant. When you're done, evenly distribute the béchamel sauce over the layers.
8. Bake until golden brown on top, about 45 minutes.
9. Before serving, give the moussaka 10 minutes to rest. If desired, garnish with fresh parsley.

Mediterranean Pork Tenderloin with Olives and Feta

Time: 45 minutes
Serving Size: 4 servings
Prep Time: 15 minutes
Cook Time: 30 minutes

Nutrition Information:

Calories: 380, Fat: 24g, Total Carbohydrate: 8g, Protein: 32g, Sodium: 620mg.

Ingredients:

- 1 pork tenderloin (about 1.5 lbs)
- 1 cup Kalamata olives, pitted and halved

- 1/2 cup crumbled feta cheese
- 2 tablespoons fresh rosemary, minced
- 2 garlic cloves, minced
- 1/4 cup olive oil
- Zest and juice of 1 lemon
- Salt and pepper, to taste
- 1/2 cup cherry tomatoes, halved
- 1 tablespoon fresh parsley, chopped (for garnish)

Directions:

1. Your oven should be preheated at 375°F (190°C).
2. In a basin, combine the olive oil, zest and juice of the lemon, garlic, rosemary, salt, and pepper.
3. Transfer the tenderloin of pork to a baking dish. Cover the pork completely by covering it with half of the olive oil mixture and then flipping it over. Save the other half for a different time.
4. Roast the pork tenderloin in the oven for around thirty minutes.
5. Scatter the cherry tomatoes, feta cheese crumbles, and Kalamata olives over the pork after taking it out of the oven.
6. Drizzle the leftover olive oil mixture over the meat and vegetables.
7. Bake for ten minutes, or until the pork reaches an internal temperature of 145°F (63°C), and the feta starts to melt.
8. After taking it out of the oven, give it five minutes to rest.
9. When the pork is sliced, it is served with the tomatoes, feta, and olives. Sprinkle some finely chopped parsley on top.

Lamb Tagine with Dates and Cinnamon

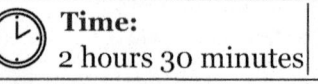
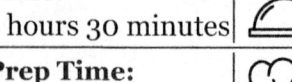

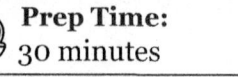

Time: 2 hours 30 minutes	Serving Size: 6 servings
Prep Time: 30 minutes	Cook Time: 2 hours

Nutrition Information:

Calories: 460, Fat: 24g, Total Carbohydrate: 33g, Protein: 32g, Sodium: 310mg.

Ingredients:

- 1.5 lbs lamb shoulder, cut into 1-inch cubes
- 1 cup Medjool dates, pitted and halved
- 2 teaspoons ground cinnamon
- 1 large onion, finely chopped
- 2 garlic cloves, minced
- 1 teaspoon ground ginger
- 1/2 teaspoon ground turmeric
- 1/4 teaspoon saffron threads
- 2 cups chicken or lamb broth
- 2 tablespoons olive oil
- 1/4 cup almond slivers, toasted
- Salt and pepper, to taste
- Fresh cilantro, for garnish
- 1 lemon, zested and juiced

Directions:

1. Add salt, pepper, and half of the cinnamon to the lamb cubes in a large bowl and mix well. Let the lamb cubes marinate for 15 minutes.
2. In a tagine or big saucepan with a heavy bottom, heat the olive oil over medium-high heat. Upon adding, brown the lamb cubes on all sides. Take out and place on the side.
3. The same pot should be used to sauté the chopped onion until it becomes translucent. Garlic, saffron, turmeric, ginger, and the remaining cinnamon should all be added. Simmer for 2 minutes, or until fragrant.
4. Go back to the saucepan with the browned

lamb. Whisk in the lemon juice and zest, then the broth (lamb or chicken). Elevate to a simmer.

5. Cover the pot or tagine, reduce the heat to low, and simmer gently for 1.5 hours.
6. Once the lamb and dates are soft, simmer for a further 20 minutes after adding the pitted dates and cooking for one hour and thirty minutes.
7. Once you taste it, adjust the seasoning.
8. With toasted almond slivers and fresh cilantro as garnishes, serve the lamb tagine hot.

Beef Kofta with Yogurt Sauce

Time: 60 minutes	Serving Size: 4 servings
Prep Time: 20 minutes	Cook Time: 40 minutes

Nutrition Information:

Calories: 280, Fat: 14g, Total Carbohydrate: 6g, Protein: 32g, Sodium: 150mg.

Ingredients:

For the Beef Kofta:

- 1 lb ground beef (lean)
- 1/4 cup fresh parsley, finely chopped
- 1 medium onion, finely chopped
- 2 garlic cloves, minced
- 1 teaspoon ground cumin
- 1 teaspoon ground coriander
- 1/2 teaspoon paprika
- 1/4 teaspoon cayenne pepper (optional, for heat)
- Salt and pepper, to taste
- 2 tablespoons olive oil

For the Yogurt Sauce:

- 1 cup plain Greek yogurt
- 1 garlic clove, minced
- 1 tablespoon fresh mint, finely chopped
- 1 tablespoon olive oil
- Salt, to taste
- 1 tablespoon lemon juice

Directions:

1. In a large mixing bowl, mix together the ground beef, parsley, onion, garlic, cumin, coriander, paprika, cayenne (if using), salt, and pepper. Till well combined, thoroughly mix.
2. After dividing the ingredients into eight equal portions, form each into an elongated sausage.
3. Over medium-high heat, preheat the olive oil in a skillet. Be cautious not to overcrowd the skillet when adding the koftas once it has heated up. On each side, sauté them for about 6–7 minutes, or until they are well cooked and browned.
4. Combine Greek yogurt, minced garlic, mint, olive oil, salt, and lemon juice in a small dish to make the yogurt sauce while the koftas cook. Blend until consistency is reached.
5. Serve the koftas hot with the yogurt sauce on the side.

Greek-style Stuffed Bell Peppers with Ground Lamb

Time: 1 hour 10 minutes	Serving Size: 4 servings
Prep Time: 20 minutes	Cook Time: 50 minutes

Nutrition Information:

Calories: 390, Fat: 24g, Total Carbohydrate: 21g, Protein: 22g, Sodium: 270mg.

Ingredients:

- 4 large bell peppers (red, yellow, or green)
- 1 lb ground lamb
- 1 cup cooked rice
- 1 medium onion, finely chopped
- 2 garlic cloves, minced
- 1 can (14 oz) diced tomatoes, drained
- 1/4 cup fresh parsley, chopped
- 1 teaspoon dried oregano
- 1/2 teaspoon ground cinnamon
- Salt and pepper, to taste
- 2 tablespoons olive oil
- 1/4 cup crumbled feta cheese
- 1/4 cup kalamata olives, pitted and chopped

Directions:

1. Set oven temperature to 375°F (190°C).
2. Slice off the tops and remove the seeds from bell peppers. Add a tiny bit of salt within.
3. Fill a big skillet with olive oil and place it over medium heat. When heated through, sauté the onions and garlic until translucent.
4. After adding, cook the lamb ground until browned. Drain the fat if more is required.
5. Add the cooked rice, chopped tomatoes, parsley, cinnamon, oregano, and salt & pepper. Allow to cook for 5 minutes to allow flavors to combine.
6. Take it off the stove and mix in the chopped olives and feta crumbles.
7. Place the lamb mixture inside each bell pepper and bake them.
8. With the foil covering, bake the dish for thirty minutes. Remove the foil and roast the peppers for 10 minutes, or until they are slightly browned and tender.
9. Before serving, take the dish out of the oven and let it rest for a while.

Spiced Pork Kebabs with Cucumber Salad

Time: 1 hour 25 minutes
Serving Size: 4 servings
Prep Time: 35 minutes
Cook Time: 50 minutes

Nutrition Information:

Calories: 280, Fat: 15g, Total Carbohydrate: 6g, Protein: 28g, Sodium: 120mg.

Ingredients:

For the Pork Kebabs:

- 1 lb pork tenderloin, cut into 1-inch cubes
- 2 tablespoons olive oil
- 2 garlic cloves, minced
- 1 teaspoon smoked paprika
- 1 teaspoon ground cumin
- 1/2 teaspoon ground coriander
- 1/4 teaspoon cayenne pepper
- Salt and pepper, to taste
- Wooden skewers, soaked in water for 30 minutes

For the Cucumber Salad:

- 1 large cucumber, thinly sliced
- 1/4 cup red onion, thinly sliced
- 1/4 cup fresh mint, chopped
- 2 tablespoons fresh lemon juice
- 2 tablespoons olive oil
- Salt and pepper, to taste

Directions:

1. In a large mixing bowl, stir together olive oil, garlic, smoked paprika, cumin, coriander, cayenne, salt, and pepper. After adding, coat the pork cubes thoroughly. Marinade for a minimum of twenty minutes.
2. Prior to the pork being marinated, prepare the cucumber salad. In a bowl, add cucumber slices, red onion slices, and fresh mint. Gently whisk together the lemon juice, olive oil, salt, and pepper in a separate small bowl.

Stir to mix after adding the dressing to the cucumber dish. Set alone to let flavors meld.

3. High heat should be applied before using a grill or grill pan. Stuff the marinated pork pieces onto the moistened skewers.

4. Cook the skewers for 7 to 9 minutes on each side, or until the pork is cooked through and has lovely grill marks.

5. The kebabs should be allowed to rest after being taken off the grill.

6. Serve the pork kebabs with the cucumber salad on the side.

Mediterranean Beef Stew with Rosemary and Tomatoes

Time: 2 hours 30 minutes	Serving Size: 6 servings
Prep Time: 30 minutes	Cook Time: 2 hours

Nutrition Information:

Calories: 320, Fat: 12g, Total Carbohydrate: 18g, Protein: 35g, Sodium: 420mg.

Ingredients:

- 2 lbs beef chuck, cut into 1-inch cubes
- 2 tablespoons olive oil
- 1 large onion, chopped
- 3 garlic cloves, minced
- 1 tablespoon tomato paste
- 1/2 cup dry red wine
- 1 can (28 oz) diced tomatoes
- 2 sprigs fresh rosemary
- 2 bay leaves
- 1 cup beef broth
- 2 carrots, sliced
- 1 bell pepper, chopped
- 1 zucchini, sliced
- Salt and pepper, to taste
- Fresh parsley, for garnish

Directions:

1. Over medium heat, warm the olive oil in a big pot or Dutch oven. Put some salt and pepper on the beef cubes. To avoid packing the pot too full, brown the beef in batches. Lift out and place the browned steak aside.

2. Add the diced onion to the same saucepan and cook it until it becomes transparent. Stir till aromatic after adding the garlic and tomato paste.

3. While scraping out any browned bits from the bottom of the pot, pour in the red wine to deglaze it. Let the wine diminish to half by simmering it.

4. Add diced tomatoes, bay leaves, rosemary sprigs, and beef stock to the pot after adding the steak back. Before lowering the heat to a simmer, bring the mixture to a boil.

5. After 30 minutes, boil the stew with a lid on.

6. Stir in the bell pepper, zucchini, and carrots. Once the beef and vegetables are fork-tender, simmer for a further thirty minutes.

7. Use salt and pepper to adjust the seasoning as necessary. Stems of rosemary and bay leaves should be removed.

8. Serve the stew in bowls, garnished with fresh parsley.

Lamb and Spinach Curry

Time: 1 hour 45 minutes	Serving Size: 4 servings
Prep Time: 15 minutes	Cook Time: 1 hour 30 minutes

Nutrition Information:

Calories: 310, Fat: 16g, Total Carbohydrate: 15g, Protein: 29g, Sodium: 220mg.

Ingredients:

- 1 lb lamb shoulder, cut into cubes
- 1 tablespoon olive oil
- 1 large onion, finely chopped
- 3 garlic cloves, minced
- 1-inch piece of fresh ginger, grated
- 2 teaspoons ground cumin
- 2 teaspoons ground coriander
- 1 teaspoon ground turmeric
- 1 teaspoon smoked paprika
- 1/2 teaspoon red chili powder (adjust to taste)
- 1 can (14 oz) diced tomatoes
- 2 cups fresh spinach, washed and roughly chopped
- 1 cup yogurt
- Salt and pepper, to taste
- Fresh cilantro, for garnish
- Lemon wedges, for serving

Directions:

1. A medium burner is used to warm the olive oil in a large pot. Brown the lamb cubes in batches so that cooking will be uniform. Remove and set aside the meat that has browned.
2. Add the chopped onion and sauté until it becomes translucent in the same pot. Add ginger and garlic and stir until fragrant, about 1 minute later.
3. Stir in paprika, red chili powder, turmeric, coriander, and ground cumin. To release their aroma, mix the spices and simmer for one minute.
4. Now that the lamb is back in the pot, toss it around to thoroughly coat it with the spice mixture.
5. Taste and add salt and pepper to taste. Add the diced tomatoes and boil the mixture.
6. You cover and reduce the heat to low-heat simmer for one hour, stirring occasionally.
7. Once the spinach has been cut, stir it into the curry and allow it to wilt. Cook for an additional fifteen minutes.
8. The curry will become creamy if you remove the pot from the heat and whisk in the yogurt.
9. Lemon wedges should be served on the side, along with fresh cilantro for garnish.

Slow-cooked Pork Shoulder with Mediterranean Herbs

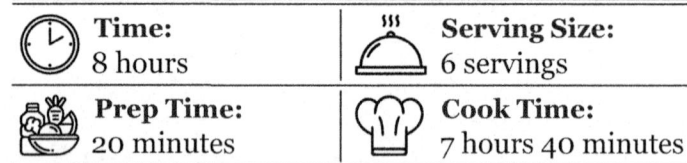

Time: 8 hours	Serving Size: 6 servings
Prep Time: 20 minutes	Cook Time: 7 hours 40 minutes

Nutrition Information:

Calories: 310, Fat: 18g, Total Carbohydrate: 6g, Protein: 28g, Sodium: 230mg.

Ingredients:

- 2.5 lbs pork shoulder
- 3 tablespoons olive oil
- 1 large onion, sliced
- 4 cloves garlic, minced
- 1 tablespoon fresh rosemary, chopped
- 1 tablespoon fresh thyme, chopped
- 2 teaspoons dried oregano
- 1 cup dry white wine
- 1 cup chicken broth
- 2 bay leaves
- 1 lemon, zested and juiced
- Salt and pepper, to taste
- Fresh parsley, for garnish

Directions:

1. Season the pork shoulder with a liberal amount of salt and pepper.
2. In a large skillet, preheat the olive oil over medium-high heat. Give the pork shoulder a nice browning. Take out and set aside.
3. Transfer the sliced onions to the same skillet

and sauté until they become translucent. Minced garlic, oregano, rosemary, and thyme. Cook for an additional two minutes.

4. After adding the white wine, boil it for a minute while scraping up any browned bits from the pan's bottom.

5. Pour the mixture of onions and herbs into a slow cooker. Top with the browned pork shoulder.

6. Cover the pork with the chicken broth. Incorporate the lemon zest, lemon juice, and bay leaves.

7. Cook on low heat for 8 hours with the cover on, or until the pork is tender and easily shreds.

8. When finished, shred the pork and combine it with the flavorful juices within the slow cooker.

9. Garnish with fresh parsley and serve warm.

Chapter 11: Desserts, Fruits Recipes

Greek Yogurt with Honey and Walnuts

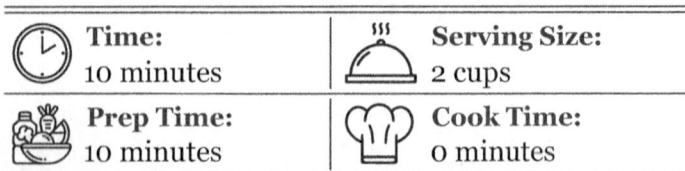

Nutrition Information:

Calories: 370, Fat: 20g, Total Carbohydrate: 31g, Protein: 20g, Sodium: 65mg.

Ingredients:

- 2 cups full-fat Greek yogurt
- 4 tablespoons raw honey
- 1/2 cup walnuts, roughly chopped
- A pinch of ground cinnamon (optional)
- Fresh fruit, for garnish (optional, such as berries or sliced banana)

Directions:

1. Spoon the Greek yogurt equally into two serving bowls.
2. Drizzle two tablespoons of raw honey over each bowl of yogurt.
3. Sprinkle the chopped walnuts over the yogurt and honey.
4. For flavor, sprinkle a pinch of ground cinnamon on top if preferred.
5. Garnish with fresh fruit if you like.
6. Serve immediately and enjoy this creamy, crunchy, and sweet delight.

Mediterranean Lemon Olive Oil Cake

Nutrition Information:

Calories: 320, Fat: 15g, Total Carbohydrate: 42g, Protein: 5g, Sodium: 220mg.

Ingredients:

- 1 3/4 cups all-purpose flour
- 2 teaspoons baking powder
- 1/2 teaspoon salt
- 1 cup granulated sugar
- Zest of 2 lemons
- 3 large eggs
- 1/2 cup extra-virgin olive oil
- 1/2 cup whole milk or almond milk
- 1/4 cup fresh lemon juice
- 1 teaspoon pure vanilla extract
- Powdered sugar, for dusting
- Fresh berries or whipped cream, for serving (optional)

Directions:

1. Heat your oven to 350 F (175 C).

2. Line a 9-inch round cake pan with parchment paper and lightly grease the surface. In a medium-sized bowl, sift together the flour, baking powder, and a pinch of salt. Set this mixture aside for later.

3. In a larger mixing bowl, blend the granulated sugar with the fragrant lemon zest, working the zest into the sugar with your fingers until the sugar is aromatic. Add the eggs to the lemon-sugar blend one by one, whisking until the mixture is homogeneous and creamy.

4. Next, fold in the olive oil slowly, and then mix in the milk, fresh lemon juice, and a splash of vanilla extract until the mixture is fully integrated. With continuous stirring, gently combine the dry ingredients with the wet mix, just until the batter is even and lump-free.

5. Pour the batter into your prepared cake pan, smoothing the surface with a spatula. Bake in the oven at the set temperature for about 50 to 55 minutes, or until a toothpick inserted into the center of the cake comes out without any wet batter.

6. Let the cake cool in the pan for a brief period, about 10 minutes, then transfer it to a cooling rack to cool down completely. Once cool, sprinkle over some powdered sugar for a sweet finish, and serve with fresh berries or a dollop of whipped cream if desired.

Fresh Fruit Salad with Mint and Lemon Drizzle

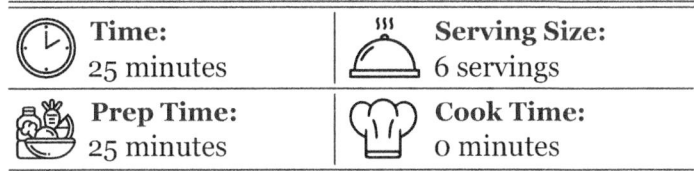

🕐	**Time:** 25 minutes	🍽	**Serving Size:** 6 servings
🥗	**Prep Time:** 25 minutes	👨‍🍳	**Cook Time:** 0 minutes

Nutrition Information:

Calories: 90, Fat: 0.5g, Total Carbohydrate: 22g, Protein: 1g, Sodium: 10mg.

Ingredients:

- 2 cups strawberries, hulled and halved
- 1 cup blueberries
- 1 cup raspberries
- 2 kiwis, peeled and sliced
- 1 orange, peeled and segmented
- 1 cup pineapple chunks
- 1/4 cup fresh mint leaves, finely chopped
- Zest and juice of 1 lemon
- 2 tablespoons honey
- Pinch of salt

Directions:

1. In a large mixing bowl, combine strawberries, blueberries, raspberries, kiwis, orange segments, and pineapple chunks. Toss gently to mix.

2. In a small bowl, whisk together the lemon zest, lemon juice, honey, and a little pinch of salt. Stir in the finely chopped mint after adding it.

3. Over the fruit in the mixing bowl, drizzle the mint and lemon mixture. To uniformly coat the fruit with the drizzle, toss gently.

4. To allow the flavors to mingle, let the fruit salad sit for approximately ten minutes.

5. If preferred, present the fruit salad in separate bowls and top with extra mint leaves.

Baklava Rolls with Pistachio and Honey

Time: 1 hour 30 minutes	Serving Size: 12 servings
Prep Time: 30 minutes	Cook Time: 60 minutes

Nutrition Information:

Calories: 210, Fat: 12g, Total Carbohydrate: 25g, Protein: 3g, Sodium: 55mg.

Ingredients:

- 1 package (16 oz) phyllo dough, thawed
- 2 cups pistachios, finely chopped
- 1 cup walnuts, finely chopped
- 3/4 cup granulated sugar
- 1 tablespoon ground cinnamon
- 1 cup unsalted butter, melted
- 1 cup honey
- 1 teaspoon vanilla extract
- Zest of 1 orange
- 1/4 teaspoon salt

Directions:

1. Preheat the oven to 350°F (175°C).
2. Toss together the walnuts, sugar, cinnamon, salt, and pistachios in a mixing dish.
3. Unroll the phyllo dough, then cut it in half. Place a moist cloth over it to keep it from drying out.
4. Melt the butter and place one phyllo sheet on top of it. Before putting another sheet on top, brush the top one with more butter.
5. Sprinkle a thin coating of the nut mixture onto the buttered phyllo.
6. Form the phyllo into a tightly rolled log with care. Cut into pieces that are one inch each. Line a baking tray with parchment paper and arrange the rolls on it.
7. Proceed with the leftover phyllo sheets and filling.
8. Place in a preheated oven and bake for 40 to 45 minutes, or until golden brown and crisp.
9. In a saucepan, mix honey, vanilla, and orange zest while the baklava rolls are baking. Simmer and allow it to cook for five to seven minutes.
10. When the baklava rolls come out of the oven, sprinkle them right away with the heated honey mixture. Before serving, let them sit for about 20 minutes to chill and soak up the syrup.

Mediterranean Almond Cookies

Time: 35 minutes	Serving Size: 10 servings
Prep Time: 15 minutes	Cook Time: 20 minutes

Nutrition Information:

Calories: 85, Fat: 6g, Total Carbohydrate: 7g, Protein: 3g, Sodium: 25mg.

Ingredients:

- 2 cups almond flour
- 1/2 cup granulated sugar
- 1/4 teaspoon salt
- 1/4 teaspoon baking soda
- Zest of 1 lemon
- Zest of 1 orange
- 1 egg
- 1 teaspoon almond extract
- 1/2 cup whole almonds, for topping
- Powdered sugar, for dusting (optional)

Directions:

1. Adjust the oven's temperature to 175 °C/350 °F. Use parchment paper to line a baking sheet if you're not using a silicone baking mat.

2. Combine almond flour, granulated sugar, salt, baking soda, and zest from the orange and lemon in a mixing dish.
3. Whisk the egg and almond extract in a separate dish until lightly frothy.
4. Gradually blend the wet mixture into the dry ingredients. Stirring will create a dough.
5. Remove the dough into twenty-four equal pieces. After carefully flattening each component, make each into a ball and set it on the baking sheet. Press a full nut into the center of each cookie.
6. After 20 to 25 minutes of baking, the edges should turn golden brown. As the cookies cool, they lose the softness that they had when they were hot.
7. The cookies should cool for ten minutes on the baking sheet, then they should be moved to a wire rack to cool completely.
8. Before serving, if preferred, sprinkle with powdered sugar.

Apricot and Almond Tart

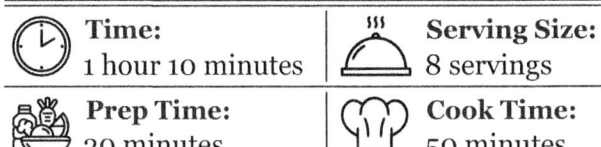

Nutrition Information:

Calories: 280, Fat: 16g, Total Carbohydrate: 30g, Protein: 5g, Sodium: 115mg.

Ingredients:

- 1 pre-made pie crust (9 inches) or homemade
- 1 cup fresh apricots, halved and pitted
- 1 cup ground almonds (almond meal)
- 1/2 cup granulated sugar
- 1/4 cup unsalted butter, softened
- 1 large egg
- 1 teaspoon almond extract
- 1/2 teaspoon vanilla extract
- 1/4 teaspoon salt
- 2 tablespoons apricot jam (for glazing)
- Slivered almonds, for garnish
- Powdered sugar, for dusting (optional)

Directions:

1. Preheat the oven to 375°F (190°C).
2. Before putting the pie crust into a 9-inch tart pan, trim off any excess dough. Prick the bottom with a fork and let it rest for about fifteen minutes.
3. In a medium-sized mixing dish, thoroughly incorporate butter and sugar. Add the nutmeg, almond, vanilla, and salt extracts. After beating, a complete blending should be obtained.
4. Once a thick paste develops, fold in the ground almonds.
5. Cover the cold pie shell with a uniform layer of the almond mixture.
6. Press the apricot halves gently down over the almond mixture after placing them, cut side up.
7. Bake for 40 to 45 minutes, or until the crust is golden brown and the filling is set.
8. In a small saucepan, heat the apricot jam until it liquidates. Strain if necessary to remove any fragments. To give the tart a glossy finish, brush the heated area on top.
9. Add some slivered almonds as a garnish and let it cool.
10. If desired, dust with confectioners' sugar prior to serving.

Fig and Walnut Halva

⏱ Time: 1 hour 20 minutes	🍽 Serving Size: 10 servings
🥗 Prep Time: 20 minutes	👨‍🍳 Cook Time: 1 hour

Nutrition Information:

Calories: 330, Fat: 16g, Total Carbohydrate: 44g, Protein: 5g, Sodium: 80mg.

Ingredients:

- 1 cup dried figs, finely chopped
- 1/2 cup walnuts, chopped
- 1 cup semolina
- 1/2 cup unsalted butter
- 1 cup sugar
- 1/2 teaspoon ground cardamom
- 1/4 teaspoon salt
- 2 cups water
- Zest of 1 lemon
- 1 teaspoon rose water (optional)
- A handful of whole walnuts and sliced figs for garnish

Directions:

1. In a saucepan over medium heat, the butter should melt. Add the semolina and roast, stirring constantly, until golden brown and aromatic with nutty notes.
2. In a separate pot, heat the cardamom, sugar, lemon zest, and water. After bringing it to a boil, simmer it for the sugar to dissolve entirely.
3. Stirring continuously to prevent lumps, slowly pour the sugar-water mixture into the roasted semolina. Very fast, the mixture will get thick.
4. Stir until the walnuts and chopped figs are uniformly distributed in the semolina mixture. For more flavor, whisk in the rose water, if using.
5. Turn off the heat once everything is properly blended and the halva begins to peel away from the pan's sides.
6. Spoon mixture into a dish or mold that has been buttered. To guarantee that the halva adopts the shape of the mold, firmly press down. Give it a half hour or so to cool.
7. The halva should come out of the mold readily once it has cooled and been inverted onto a plate.
8. Add sliced figs and whole walnuts as garnish.
9. Slice and serve.

Orange and Rose Water Sorbet

⏱ Time: 2 hours 30 minutes	🍽 Serving Size: 8 servings
🥗 Prep Time: 15 minutes	👨‍🍳 Cook Time: 2 hours 15 minutes

Nutrition Information:

Calories: 130, Fat: 0g, Total Carbohydrate: 33g, Protein: 0.5g, Sodium: 25mg.

Ingredients:

- 2 cups fresh orange juice (about 4-6 oranges)
- Zest of 1 orange
- 1 cup granulated sugar
- 1 cup water
- 2 tablespoons rose water
- 1 tablespoon fresh lemon juice
- A pinch of salt

Directions:

1. In a pan, mix the sugar and water together. Reduce the heat to medium and simmer, stirring occasionally, until the sugar melts. The outcome will be simple syrup. Turn off the heat and let it cool.
2. Combine the fresh orange juice, orange zest, lemon juice, and a little teaspoon of salt with

the cooled simple syrup.

3. Incorporate the rose water by stirring. Depending on your taste, alter the sweetness or rose water.
4. The mixture should be poured onto a shallow dish and placed in the freezer.
5. Once the edges begin to freeze, about 1 hour has passed. Use a fork to stir the liquid, breaking up any frozen bits.
6. After the sorbet is solid and completely frozen, put it back in the freezer and repeat the process every 30 minutes for two to three hours.
7. When set through, scoop into dishes and serve immediately.

Mediterranean Date Balls with Coconut

Time: 40 minutes	Serving Size: 12 servings
Prep Time: 30 minutes	Cook Time: 10 minutes

Nutrition Information:

Calories: 70, Fat: 2.5g, Total Carbohydrate: 11g, Protein: 1g, Sodium: 5mg.

Ingredients:

- 1 cup Medjool dates, pitted
- 1/2 cup unsalted almonds
- 1/4 cup unsweetened shredded coconut, plus extra for rolling
- 1 tablespoon chia seeds
- 1 tablespoon honey or maple syrup
- 1 teaspoon vanilla extract
- A pinch of sea salt

Directions:

1. In a food processor, combine the Medjool dates, almonds, 1/4 cup coconut flakes, chia seeds, honey or maple syrup, vanilla essence, and a pinch of salt.
2. Blend the contents until a cohesive, sticky dough is formed. If the mixture seems too dry, add a couple more dates or honey. If it's too moist, add more coconut or almonds.
3. Once everything is well combined, take a tablespoon or so of the dough and roll it between your palms to make a ball.
4. Roll each ball in the excess shredded coconut to ensure it is well covered.
5. Arrange the coated date balls on a parchment paper-covered tray.
6. Please refrigerate the date balls for a minimum of five minutes in order for them to solidify.
7. Store in an airtight jar in the refrigerator for up to 1 week.

Pistachio Pudding with Saffron

Time: 1 hour 10 minutes	Serving Size: 6 servings
Prep Time: 20 minutes	Cook Time: 50 minutes

Nutrition Information:

Calories: 180, Fat: 8g, Total Carbohydrate: 23g, Protein: 6g, Sodium: 45mg.

Ingredients:

- 2 cups whole milk
- 1/4 cup sugar
- 1 pinch of saffron threads
- 1/2 cup ground pistachios, plus additional for garnish
- 3 tablespoons cornstarch
- 1/4 cup water
- 1 teaspoon vanilla extract
- A pinch of salt

CHAPTER 11: DESSERTS, FRUITS RECIPES

Directions:

1. One tablespoon of hot milk should be used to dissolve the saffron threads in a small basin. Give it ten minutes to sit.

2. The milk should be warmed but not boiled in a saucepan over medium heat. After adding the sugar, stir until it dissolves completely.

3. To make sure the mixture is smooth, gradually add the ground pistachios to the milk while stirring continuously.

4. To make a smooth paste, combine cornstarch and water in a different basin. To prevent any lumps, stir this slowly into the combination of milk and pistachios.

5. Cook the pudding over medium heat, stirring constantly, for 7 to 10 minutes, or until it thickens and coats the back of a spoon.

6. Take off the stove and mix in the saffron milk and vanilla extract. To guarantee a consistent flavor throughout, thoroughly mix.

7. Spoon the pudding into one big dish or into individual serving dishes. After allowing them to get to room temperature, place them in the refrigerator and let them be there for at least half an hour or until the pudding sets.

8. Before serving, garnish with additional ground pistachios.

Chapter 12: Beverages

Mint and Cucumber Infused Water

Nutrition Information:

Calories: 0, Fat: 0g, Total Carbohydrate: 0g, Protein: 0g, Sodium: 0mg.

Ingredients:

- 1 medium cucumber, thinly sliced
- 10-12 fresh mint leaves, slightly crushed to release flavor
- 6 cups of purified water
- Ice cubes (optional)
- 1 lemon (optional, for added zesty flavor)

Directions:

1. Check that the cucumber and mint leaves are clean by giving them a thorough wash to get rid of any dirt or leftovers.
2. To a large pitcher, add the cucumber slices cut thinly and the crushed mint leaves.
3. Slice the lemon thinly and add it to the pitcher if you're using it to enhance flavor.
4. Fill the pitcher with the filtered water, then add the cucumber slices and mint leaves.
5. Mix the components with a gentle stir.
6. Cool the pitcher for a minimum of two to three hours after covering it. This lets the flavors combine and infuse the water with the taste of mint and cucumber.
7. Pour into cold glasses; garnish with ice cubes, if preferred.

Mediterranean Iced Coffee with Almond Milk

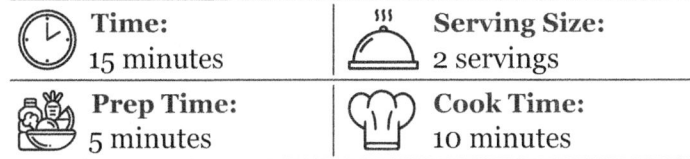

Nutrition Information:

Calories: 50, Fat: 1.5g, Total Carbohydrate: 9g, Protein: 1g, Sodium: 80mg.

Ingredients:

- 2 cups of cold brew coffee or strong brewed coffee, cooled
- 1 cup of unsweetened almond milk
- 1-2 tbsp of honey or agave syrup (adjust to taste)
- 1 tsp of vanilla extract
- 1/4 tsp ground cinnamon
- Ice cubes
- Cocoa powder for garnish (optional)
- Slivered almonds for garnish (optional)

Directions:

1. First, put some coffee in the pot. Make preparations in advance if you plan to use the cold brew method. If using ordinary brewed coffee, refrigerate it to cool it more quickly or let it cool to room temperature.
2. In a saucepan over low to medium heat, preheat the almond milk. Do not allow it to boil; you only need it heated enough to dissolve the honey or agave syrup.
3. Add honey or agave syrup to warm almond milk and whisk until all of the syrup is dissolved.
4. When you take it off the heat, add the vanilla extract and cinnamon powder.
5. Fill two large glasses with ice cubes.
6. Fill the glasses about two-thirds of the way to the top when the coffee has cooled.
7. Pour a small amount of the blended almond milk into each glass and let it emulsify with the coffee.
8. If preferred, add a small sprinkling of chocolate powder and slivered almonds as garnish.
9. Give it a moderate whirl and serve straight away.

Fresh Pomegranate and Orange Juice

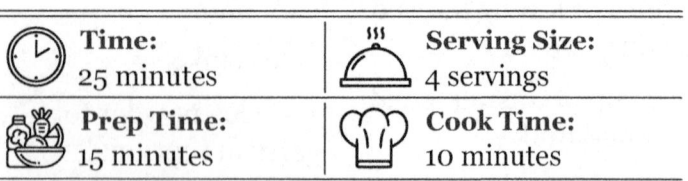

Nutrition Information:

Calories: 130, Fat: 1g, Total Carbohydrate: 31g, Protein: 2g, Sodium: 25mg.

Ingredients:

- 2 large pomegranates
- 4 medium oranges
- 1 tbsp of honey or agave syrup (optional)
- A pinch of salt
- Fresh mint leaves for garnish (optional)

Directions:

1. Halve the pomegranates. Use a citrus press by hand or a juice extractor to extract the juice from the pomegranate seeds. The seeds can be manually removed and pressed through a fine-mesh filter to get the juice if you don't have a juicer.
2. The oranges should also be sliced in half so that the juice may be extracted.
3. Strain the orange and pomegranate juices and place them in a pitcher.
4. If you would want it sweeter, mix thoroughly and add honey or agave syrup.
5. Repeatedly whisk gently after adding a pinch of salt. The fruits' inherent sweetness may be accentuated by this dash of salt.
6. When serving, immediately pour the juice into glasses and, if wanted, garnish with fresh mint leaves.

Greek Mountain Tea with Lemon and Honey

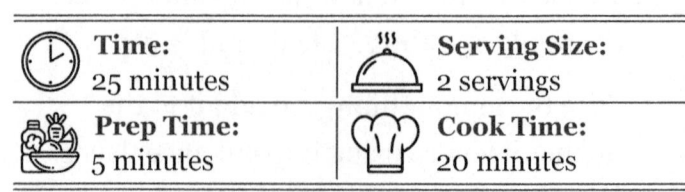

Nutrition Information:

Calories: 45, Fat: 0g, Total Carbohydrate: 12g, Protein: 0g, Sodium: 10mg.

Ingredients:

2 tbsp dried Greek mountain tea (also known as «Sideritis» or «Ironwort»)

4 cups of water

1 lemon, sliced

2 tbsp honey, or to taste

Directions:

1. Heat the water in a big saucepan or teapot until it boils.
2. After it boils, turn off the heat and stir in the dried Greek mountain tea leaves.
3. Depending on the strength you want, let the tea steep for around ten minutes.
4. After straining the tea to get rid of the leaves, transfer it to serving cups.
5. In each mug, place a piece of lemon.
6. Taste and adjust with honey to sweeten to your liking.
7. Serve hot and enjoy!

Sparkling Rosemary Limeade

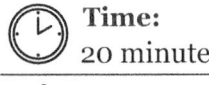 **Time:** 20 minutes **Serving Size:** 4 servings

 Prep Time: 5 minutes **Cook Time:** 15 minutes

Nutrition Information:

Calories: 90, Fat: 0g, Total Carbohydrate: 24g, Protein: 0.2g, Sodium: 25mg.

Ingredients:

- 1 cup freshly squeezed lime juice (about 8-10 limes)
- 1/2 cup sugar (or adjust to taste)
- 2 cups sparkling water or club soda
- 2 sprigs of fresh rosemary
- 1 cup water
- Lime slices and rosemary sprigs for garnish

Directions:

1. Heat the water, sugar, and two rosemary sprigs in a small saucepan. Melt the sugar over medium-low heat, stirring constantly, until it dissolves entirely. As such, simple syrup is flavored with rosemary.
2. The rosemary flavor will be added after the mixture is brought to a medium simmer and cooked for approximately ten minutes.
3. Let the syrup cool in the pot after turning off the heat. When the food has cooled, remove and discard the rosemary sprigs.
4. Pour together the freshly squeezed lime juice and the rosemary-infused simple syrup in a large pitcher. Make sure to mix fully.
5. When serving, gently stir the mixture with a pour of sparkling water or club soda.
6. Garnish with lime slices and a rosemary sprig, then serve the limeade over ice.

Mediterranean Herbal Tea Blend

 Time: 30 minutes **Serving Size:** 2 servings

 Prep Time: 10 minutes **Cook Time:** 20 minutes

Nutrition Information:

Calories: 2, Fat: 0g, Total Carbohydrate: 0.5g, Protein: 0g, Sodium: 8mg.

Ingredients:

- 1 tablespoon dried rose petals
- 1 tablespoon dried chamomile flowers
- 1 tablespoon dried lemon balm leaves
- 1 tablespoon dried lavender buds
- 1 tablespoon dried mint leaves
- 1 teaspoon dried licorice root (optional)

- 4 cups boiling water
- Honey or sweetener of choice (optional)
- Lemon slices (optional for garnish)

Directions:

1. The dried rose petals, chamomile flowers, lavender buds, mint leaves, lemon balm leaves, and licorice root (if using) should all be combined in a mixing basin. To guarantee a uniform dispersion, carefully mix them.
2. The mixture should be kept out of direct sunlight in an airtight container. to preserve the taste and fragrant characteristics of the herbs
3. Use one teaspoon of the Mediterranean Herbal Tea Blend for each cup of hot water while making the tea. Pour the mixture into a teapot or a tea infuser.
4. Pour boiling water into the herbal blend. To steep, give it 8 to 10 minutes. The longer you steep it, the more intense the flavor.
5. Once brewed, remove the tea infuser or drain it to remove the herbs. Fill the teapot with cups of tea.
6. Add honey or your preferred sweetener to taste, if desired. As a garnish, feel free to include a piece of lemon.

Iced Hibiscus and Rose Tea

Time: 30 minutes	Serving Size: 4 servings
Prep Time: 10 minutes	Cook Time: 20 minutes

Nutrition Information:

Calories: 25, Fat: 0g, Total Carbohydrate: 7g, Protein: 0g, Sodium: 10mg.

Ingredients:

- 4 cups water
- 3 tablespoons dried hibiscus flowers
- 2 tablespoons dried rose petals
- 1-2 tablespoons honey or agave nectar (adjust to taste)
- 1 lemon, juiced
- Ice cubes
- Fresh mint leaves and rose petals for garnish (optional)

Directions:

1. Heat a medium saucepan of water to a rolling boil.
2. Simmer for a few minutes, then remove from the fire and mix in the dried hibiscus and rose petals. The mixture should soak for ten to fifteen minutes with the pan covered.
3. Remove the used flowers and petals from the tea and strain it into a pitcher after it has steeped.
4. Shake the boiling tea well to fully dissolve the honey or agave nectar. Keep the tea warm until it is room temperature.
5. Incorporate the just extracted lemon juice when it has cooled.
6. Before serving, put ice cubes in glasses. Transfer the rose tea and hibiscus to the ice tray. Should you choose, garnish with a sprig of mint and a few rose petals.
7. You should utilize any leftover tea within two to three days of refrigerating it.

Lemon and Mint Cooler

⏰ Time: 25 minutes	🍽 Serving Size: 4 servings
🥗 Prep Time: 5 minutes	👨‍🍳 Cook Time: 20 minutes

Nutrition Information:

Calories: 45, Fat: 0g, Total Carbohydrate: 12g, Protein: 0g, Sodium: 5mg.

Ingredients:

- 4 cups of cold water
- 2 large lemons, juiced
- 10-12 fresh mint leaves, plus extra for garnish
- 3-4 tablespoons honey or agave nectar (adjust to taste)
- 1 cup ice cubes
- Lemon slices, for garnish
- Sparkling water (optional)

Directions:

1. In a pan, preheat 1 cup of water. Remove from the fire and stir in the honey or agave nectar until it's warm but not boiling. Simple syrup is produced as a result. Let cool until room temperature is reached.
2. Toss the lemon juice, simple syrup (honey water), and remaining 3 cups cold water together in a big pitcher. Well-mix.
3. Use a muddler or the back of a spoon to gently crush the mint leaves, releasing their oils. Pour them into the pitcher.
4. After that, stir the pitcher with the ice cubes.
5. Garnish with a lemon slice and an additional mint leaf before serving the cooler from the glasses. Finally, add a spritz of sparkling water for a fizzy variety.
6. For best freshness, serve cold and eat the same day.

Olive Leaf Tea

⏰ Time: 15 minutes	🍽 Serving Size: 2 servings
🥗 Prep Time: 5 minutes	👨‍🍳 Cook Time: 10 minutes

Nutrition Information:

Calories: 2, Fat: 0g, Total Carbohydrate: 0.5g, Protein: 0g, Sodium: 10mg.

Ingredients:

- 2 tablespoons dried olive leaves (preferably organic)
- 4 cups of water
- Optional: 1 teaspoon honey or agave nectar for sweetness
- Optional: a slice of lemon or a sprinkle of cinnamon for added flavor

Directions:

1. Put the dried olive leaves in a heat-resistant container or teapot.
2. Place the 4 cups of water in a pot and bring to a boil. Cover the olive leaves with the boiling water.
3. After placing a lid on the teapot or other container, let the tea steep for ten to fifteen minutes.
4. After discarding the olive leaves, strain the tea into mugs.
5. If preferred, add cinnamon, lemon slices, honey, or agave nectar to taste. Mix thoroughly and savor warm.
6. Remark: An age-old Mediterranean beverage with potential health benefits is olive-leaf tea. It is reported to have anti-inflammatory and antioxidant-rich qualities. The flavor of this tea is mildly bitter but calming. To suit your tastes, add more sweets or flavorings as needed.

Greek Frappe Coffee

Time: 5 minutes	Serving Size: 1 servings
Prep Time: 3 minutes	Cook Time: 2 minutes

Nutrition Information:

Calories: 30 (without milk, with milk will vary based on type), Fat: 0g, Total Carbohydrate: 8g, Protein: 0g, Sodium: 4mg.

Ingredients:

- 2 teaspoons instant coffee
- 2 teaspoons sugar (adjust to taste)
- 2 teaspoons cold water
- Ice cubes
- 1/2 cup cold water or milk (skimmed, full-fat, almond, or soy milk based on preference)

Directions:

1. In a tall glass, mix instant coffee, sugar, and two teaspoons of cold water.
2. Using a frother or small hand mixer, vigorously whisk the ingredients until it becomes creamy and foamy. Two to three minutes will pass.
3. Ice cubes should be added to the glass, leaving about an inch at the top.
4. Carefully add the extra cold water or milk, being careful not to overturn the layer of frothy coffee on top.
5. Serve with a straw, or stir gently if preferred. Savor the delightfully sparkling and delicious Greek Frappe Coffee!

Chapter 13: Bonus

DASH Herb-Baked Chicken Breasts

Time: 45 minutes	Serving Size: 4 servings
Prep Time: 15 minutes	Cook Time: 30 minutes

Nutrition Information:

Calories: 220, Fat: 9g, Total Carbohydrate: 3g, Protein: 30g, Sodium: 180mg.

Ingredients:

- 4 boneless, skinless chicken breasts
- 2 tbsp olive oil
- 2 cloves garlic, minced
- 1 tsp dried rosemary
- 1 tsp dried thyme
- 1 tsp dried oregano
- 1/4 tsp black pepper
- 1/4 tsp salt (optional, or to taste for DASH dieters)
- Zest and juice of 1 lemon
- 1/2 cup low-sodium chicken broth

Directions:

1. Set the oven's temperature to 375°F (190°C).
2. Incorporate the olive oil, finely chopped garlic, rosemary, thyme, oregano, lemon zest, lemon juice, black pepper, and salt (if desired).
3. Make sure to coat the chicken breasts thoroughly by rubbing them with the herb mixture.
4. Heat one tablespoon of olive oil in a large ovenproof skillet over medium heat. Sear chicken breasts for two to three minutes on each side, or until cooked through and golden brown.
5. Pour the chicken stock over the chicken breasts in the skillet.
6. Bake the pan for 20 to 25 minutes, or until the chicken is cooked through and the middle is no longer pink.
7. Spoon some of the skillet juices over the chicken breasts.

Quinoa & Vegetable Medley Salad

Time: 30 minutes	Serving Size: 4 servings
Prep Time: 15 minutes	Cook Time: 15 minutes

Nutrition Information:

Calories: 220, Fat: 8g, Total Carbohydrate: 32g, Protein: 8g, Sodium: 150mg.

Ingredients:

- 1 cup uncooked quinoa
- 2 cups water

- 1 cup cherry tomatoes, halved
- 1 cucumber, diced
- 1 red bell pepper, chopped
- 1/2 red onion, finely chopped
- 1/4 cup fresh parsley, chopped
- 1/4 cup fresh mint, chopped
- 2 tbsp olive oil
- 2 tbsp fresh lemon juice
- 1/4 tsp black pepper
- 1/4 tsp salt (optional for DASH dieters)

Directions:

1. Bring water to a boil in a pan. After adding the quinoa and lowering the heat to low, cover the pan, and simmer it for about 15 minutes, or until it is cooked through and the water has been absorbed. Seek for a cooler environment.
2. In a large bowl, mix together the chilled quinoa, cherry tomatoes, cucumber, bell pepper, red onion, parsley, and mint.
3. In a small bowl, mix together olive oil, lemon juice, black pepper, and salt (if using). Add the dressing and toss with the quinoa and veggie mixture.
4. To enable the flavors to meld, chill the salad for approximately one hour prior to serving.
5. Serve chilled.

Spinach and Feta Stuffed Tilapia

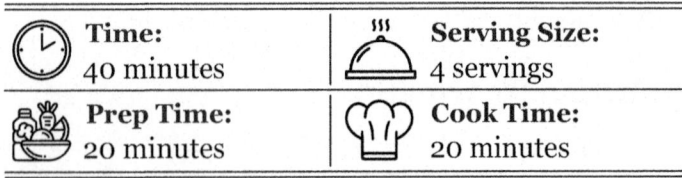

Time: 40 minutes	Serving Size: 4 servings
Prep Time: 20 minutes	Cook Time: 20 minutes

Nutrition Information:

Calories: 210, Fat: 9g, Total Carbohydrate: 3g, Protein: 29g, Sodium: 340mg.

Ingredients:

- 4 tilapia fillets (about 5-6 ounces each)
- 2 cups fresh spinach, finely chopped
- 3/4 cup crumbled feta cheese
- 2 garlic cloves, minced
- 1 tbsp olive oil
- 1 tsp lemon zest
- 2 tbsp lemon juice
- Salt and pepper, to taste (remember to keep sodium low for DASH diet compliance)
- 1/4 tsp dried oregano
- Cooking spray or olive oil for brushing

Directions:

1. Set oven temperature to 375°F (190°C).
2. In a sauté pan set over medium heat, melt the olive oil. Add the garlic and simmer, stirring, for about 1 minute, or until it begins to release its aroma.
3. Add the spinach and heat until it wilts in the pan. After taking it off the heat source, let it cool for a minute.
4. Toss the feta cheese, wilted spinach, lemon zest, lemon juice, oregano, salt, and pepper in a mixing dish. After combining, thoroughly combine.
5. Arrange the feta and spinach mixture evenly over one half of each flattened tilapia fillet. Fold the remaining half over to cover the mixture.
6. After lightly brushing the stuffed tilapia fillets with olive oil or cooking spray, place them in a baking dish.
7. After preheating the oven, cook the tilapia for fifteen to twenty minutes, or until it flakes easily with a fork.
8. Serve hot, garnished with additional lemon slices if desired.

DASH-friendly Whole Wheat Spaghetti with Fresh Tomato Sauce

Time: 25 minutes	Serving Size: 4 servings
Prep Time: 10 minutes	Cook Time: 15 minutes

Nutrition Information:

Calories: 280, Fat: 8g, Total Carbohydrate: 46g, Protein: 11g, Sodium: 150mg.

Ingredients:

- 8 oz whole wheat spaghetti
- 4 ripe tomatoes, diced
- 2 garlic cloves, minced
- 1 onion, finely chopped
- 1 bell pepper, diced (color of choice)
- 2 tbsp olive oil
- 1/4 cup fresh basil, chopped
- 1/4 cup fresh parsley, chopped
- 1/4 tsp black pepper
- 1/2 tsp dried oregano
- 1/4 tsp salt (optional for DASH dieters)
- 1/4 cup grated Parmesan cheese (optional)

Directions:

1. Cook the whole wheat spaghetti as directed on the package in a big saucepan of boiling water. After draining, set away.
2. Heat the olive oil in a big skillet over a medium heat setting. Add the garlic and onions and sauté until they are translucent.
3. Sauté the bell pepper for an additional two to three minutes after adding it.
4. After adding the diced tomatoes, boil the mixture for twenty minutes. Stir from time to time.
5. To the sauce, add the oregano, black pepper, and salt (if using). Cook for a further five minutes.
6. Stir in the parsley and fresh basil, then remove from the heat and set aside.
7. Serve the fresh tomato sauce over the cooked spaghetti. Top with grated Parmesan cheese if desired.

Almond Berry Overnight Oats

Time: 15 minutes	Serving Size: 2 servings
Prep Time: 10 minutes	Cook Time: 5 minutes

Nutrition Information:

Calories: 310, Fat: 9g, Total Carbohydrate: 50g, Protein: 10g, Sodium: 170mg.

Ingredients:

- 1 cup rolled oats
- 2 cups unsweetened almond milk
- 1/2 cup mixed berries (blueberries, raspberries, strawberries)
- 2 tbsp chia seeds
- 1 tbsp honey or maple syrup (adjust to taste)
- 1/4 cup sliced almonds
- 1/2 tsp vanilla extract
- Pinch of salt

Directions:

1. Combine rolled oats, chia seeds, vanilla extract, and a small amount of salt in a bowl.
2. Stir with your preferred sweetener (maple syrup or honey) and almond milk. Mix thoroughly until evenly distributed.
3. Half of the sliced almonds and the mixed berries should be folded in.
4. Transfer the mixture into two jars or containers that have a lid that fits tightly.
5. Refrigerate the jars for at least eight hours or overnight after sealing them.
6. Stir the oats thoroughly before serving. You

can adjust the consistency by adding a small amount of additional almond milk if the mixture is too thick.

7. Top with the remaining sliced almonds and some fresh berries.

Slow-Cooked Lentil Soup with Vegetables

⏰ Time: 8 hours 30 minutes	🍲 Serving Size: 6 servings
🥗 Prep Time: 30 minutes	👨‍🍳 Cook Time: 8 hours

Nutrition Information:

Calories: 210, Fat: 4g, Total Carbohydrate: 33g, Protein: 12g, Sodium: 220mg.

Ingredients:

- 1 cup dry green lentils, rinsed and drained
- 4 cups vegetable broth (low sodium)
- 2 cups water
- 1 large carrot, diced
- 2 celery stalks, diced
- 1 medium onion, chopped
- 2 cloves garlic, minced
- 1 medium zucchini, diced
- 1 red bell pepper, chopped
- 2 bay leaves
- 1/2 tsp dried thyme
- 1/2 tsp dried oregano
- Salt and pepper to taste (remember to keep sodium levels low)
- 2 tbsp olive oil
- 2 cups chopped fresh spinach or kale

Directions:

1. In your slow cooker, combine lentils, vegetable broth, water, bell pepper, carrot, celery, onion, garlic, and oregano.
2. Stir in the olive oil and stir again to mix.
3. Lentils and veggies should be soft after 7 to 8 hours of low-temperature cooking under cover.
4. Add salt and pepper to taste and season the soup about half an hour before serving. Recall that the objective is to control salt levels, so use caution while adding.
5. As the soup warms up, add the chopped spinach or kale and stir.
6. Discard bay leaves before serving.

Honey Garlic Chicken with Carrots and Broccoli

⏰ Time: 45 minutes	🍲 Serving Size: 4 servings
🥗 Prep Time: 15 minutes	👨‍🍳 Cook Time: 30 minutes

Nutrition Information:

Calories: 360, Fat: 6g, Total Carbohydrate: 40g, Protein: 35g, Sodium: 490mg.

Ingredients:

- 4 boneless, skinless chicken breasts
- 1/3 cup honey
- 4 cloves garlic, minced
- 1/2 cup low-sodium soy sauce
- 1/4 cup ketchup
- 1 tbsp olive oil
- 1/2 tsp dried oregano
- 1/2 tsp dried basil
- Salt and pepper to taste
- 2 medium carrots, sliced into thin rounds
- 2 cups broccoli florets
- 1 tbsp cornstarch (for thickening, optional)
- 2 tbsp cold water (for thickening, optional)
- Chopped fresh parsley or green onions for garnish

Directions:

1. In a mixing bowl, mix together the honey, garlic powder, soy sauce, ketchup, oregano, basil, salt, and pepper.
2. Place the chicken breasts in the slow cooker

bottom-up. Over the chicken, drizzle the honey-garlic mixture.

3. Divide the chopped carrots among the chicken's surrounds.
4. Cook for 5 hours on low with a cover on.
5. Broccoli florets should be added to the slow cooker after five hours.
6. Make sure the broccoli is well covered with sauce by giving it a little stir.
7. Let the food cook for another hour.
8. To make a thicker sauce, whisk together cornflour and cold water in a small basin. Stir the thickened sauce into the slow cooker, cover, and cook for an additional 10 to 15 minutes on high.
9. Before serving, garnish with fresh parsley or green onions.

Crockpot Vegetable and Bean Chili

 Time: 8 hours 35 minutes **Serving Size:** 8 servings
 **Prep Time:** 35 minutes **Cook Time:** 8 hours

Nutrition Information:

Calories: 240, Fat: 3g, Total Carbohydrate: 45g, Protein: 12g, Sodium: 450mg.

Ingredients:

- 1 cup diced bell peppers (mixed colors)
- 1 medium onion, diced
- 2 medium carrots, diced
- 3 garlic cloves, minced
- 1 can (15 oz) black beans, drained and rinsed
- 1 can (15 oz) kidney beans, drained and rinsed
- 1 can (15 oz) diced tomatoes, undrained
- 1 can (6 oz) tomato paste
- 2 cups vegetable broth
- 2 tsp ground cumin
- 1 tsp smoked paprika
- 1 tsp dried oregano
- 1/4 tsp cayenne pepper (adjust to taste)
- Salt and black pepper to taste
- 1 cup frozen corn kernels
- 2 tbsp fresh cilantro, chopped (for garnish)
- 1 avocado, sliced (optional, for serving)

Directions:

1. In the slow cooker, combine the bell peppers, onion, carrots, garlic, kidney beans, black beans, diced tomatoes, tomato paste, vegetable broth, dried oregano, smoked paprika, ground cumin, cayenne pepper, salt, and black pepper. Make a good stir.
2. For 7.5 hours, cook on low with a cover on.
3. Add the frozen corn kernels and mix. After 30 minutes, or until the corn is thoroughly heated, keep cooking.
4. If needed, taste and adjust the seasoning.
5. Serve hot, garnished with fresh cilantro and slices of avocado if desired.

Savory Pot Roast with Root Vegetables

 Time: 4 hours 20 minutes **Serving Size:** 6 servings
 Prep Time: 20 minutes **Cook Time:** 4 hours

Nutrition Information:

Calories: 450, Fat: 20g, Total Carbohydrate: 30g, Protein: 35g, Sodium: 500mg.

Ingredients:

- 2.5 lbs boneless beef chuck roast
- 2 medium carrots, sliced
- 2 parsnips, sliced
- 1 large onion,

- chopped
- 2 medium potatoes, diced
- 3 garlic cloves, minced
- 1 tsp salt
- 1/2 tsp black pepper
- 2 tsp dried thyme
- 1 tsp dried rosemary
- 1 cup beef broth (preferably low-sodium)
- 1/4 cup red wine (optional)
- 1 tbsp olive oil
- 2 tbsp tomato paste
- 2 tbsp Worcestershire sauce
- 1 bay leaf

Directions:

1. Before cooking the beef chuck roast, season it with salt and pepper.
2. The olive oil should be warmed in a skillet over medium-high heat. The roast should be inserted and seared for 4 minutes, or until browned on each side. Place within the slow cooker.
3. Scoop off any browned parts and use the same skillet to deglaze with a small amount of beef stock. After adding the Worcestershire sauce and tomato paste, stir everything together. Drizzle the roast with this mixture from the slow cooker.
4. Add sliced onion, parsnips, cubed potatoes, and carrots to the roast's surroundings.
5. Over the meat and veggies, scatter the rosemary, thyme, and garlic. Incorporate the bay leaf.
6. Cover the contents of the slow cooker with the beef broth and the red wine, if using.
7. Once the vegetables are thoroughly cooked and the beef is soft, cover and simmer on low for around nine to ten hours.
8. Discard the bay leaf before serving.

Creamy Butternut Squash Soup

Nutrition Information:

Calories: 190, Fat: 8g, Total Carbohydrate: 28g, Protein: 3g, Sodium: 350mg.

Ingredients:

- 1 large butternut squash (about 3 lbs), peeled, seeded, and diced
- 1 medium onion, chopped
- 2 carrots, sliced
- 2 garlic cloves, minced
- 4 cups chicken or vegetable broth (preferably low-sodium)
- 1 cup coconut milk or light cream
- 1/2 tsp salt (adjust to taste)
- 1/4 tsp black pepper
- 1/2 tsp nutmeg
- 1 tsp cinnamon
- 1 tbsp olive oil
- Fresh parsley or chives for garnish (optional)

Directions:

1. In a skillet over medium heat, sauté the onions in the olive oil until they become translucent. Incorporate the garlic and cook for a further minute.
2. Move the onion and garlic to the slow cooker and add the chopped butternut squash, sliced carrots, salt, pepper, cinnamon, and nutmeg.
3. Pour the chicken or vegetable broth over the vegetables in the slow cooker.
4. Vegetables should be cooked for 6–7 hours on low, covered, or until soft.
5. Once heated, transfer the soup, in batches, to a conventional blender and purée it there with an immersion blender until it's smooth.
6. Cook on low for an additional fifteen minutes, stirring in the light cream or coconut milk,

until heated through.

7. If necessary, taste and adjust the seasonings.
8. If preferred, top with fresh chives or parsley before serving.

Air-Fried Parmesan Zucchini Sticks

⏱ Time: 35 minutes	🍽 Serving Size: 4 servings
🥗 Prep Time: 15 minutes	👨‍🍳 Cook Time: 20 minutes

Nutrition Information:

Calories: 140, Fat: 7g, Total Carbohydrate: 10g, Protein: 8g, Sodium: 220mg.

Ingredients:

- 2 medium-sized zucchinis
- 1/2 cup grated Parmesan cheese
- 1/2 cup almond flour or breadcrumbs
- 1 tsp dried oregano
- 1/2 tsp garlic powder
- Salt and black pepper to taste
- 2 large eggs, beaten
- Cooking spray

Directions:

1. Set your air fryer's temperature to 375°F (190°C).
2. Make sure the zucchini sticks are cut evenly in length.
3. Mix the Parmesan cheese, bread crumbs or almond flour, garlic powder, oregano, salt, and pepper in a mixing bowl.
4. Shake off any excess egg before dipping each zucchini stick into the beaten egg mixture.
5. Press the Parmesan mixture onto each stick so that it sticks together.
6. Making sure they are not in contact with one another, arrange the coated zucchini sticks in the air fryer basket in a single layer.
7. Use a small amount of frying spray on the zucchini sticks.
8. Fry for 12 to 15 minutes in the air fryer, rotating them halfway through, or until they are crispy and golden brown.
9. Remove from the air fryer and serve immediately with your favorite dipping sauce.

Crispy Air Fryer Lemon Pepper Chicken Wings

⏱ Time: 60 minutes	🍽 Serving Size: 4 servings
🥗 Prep Time: 10 minutes	👨‍🍳 Cook Time: 50 minutes

Nutrition Information:

Calories: 290, Fat: 20g, Total Carbohydrate: 3g, Protein: 24g, Sodium: 640mg.

Ingredients:

- 2 lbs chicken wings, separated into flats and drumettes
- Zest and juice of 2 lemons
- 2 tbsp black pepper, freshly ground
- 1 tsp salt
- 1 tsp garlic powder
- 1 tbsp olive oil
- Fresh parsley for garnish (optional)
- Lemon wedges for serving

Directions:

1. In a large mixing bowl, whisk together the lemon zest, lemon juice, olive oil, salt, freshly ground black pepper, and garlic powder. Mix thoroughly.
2. Add the chicken wings to the basin and toss them with the lemon-pepper mixture. Allow them to marinate for about ten minutes.

3. Adjust the temperature on the air fryer to 380°F (190°C).

4. When placing the chicken wings in the air fryer basket in a single layer, please make sure they do not overlap.

5. Cook the wings for 20 to 25 minutes, rotating them halfway through, or until they are crispy on the outside and golden brown.

6. After that, move the wings to a platter for serving.

7. Serve with lemon wedges on the side and garnish with fresh parsley.

Golden-Brown Air Fryer Potato Wedges

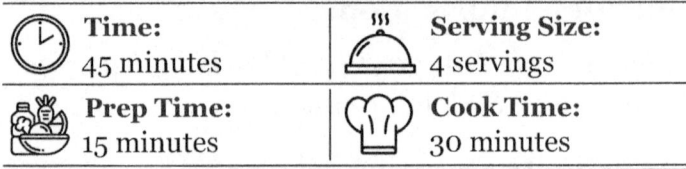

Nutrition Information:

Calories: 210, Fat: 7g, Total Carbohydrate: 35g, Protein: 4g, Sodium: 590mg.

Ingredients:

- 4 large russet potatoes, scrubbed and cut into wedges
- 2 tbsp olive oil
- 1 tsp garlic powder
- 1 tsp onion powder
- 1 tsp paprika
- 1/2 tsp ground black pepper
- 1 tsp sea salt, plus extra for finishing
- Optional: fresh chopped parsley and grated Parmesan cheese for garnish

Directions:

1. In a large plate, soak potato wedges in cold water for approximately ten minutes. The additional starch is removed, which makes the potatoes crispier.

2. After draining, pat the potatoes dry with paper towels.

3. Mix the olive oil, sea salt, paprika, onion, garlic, and black pepper in the same bowl. When the dry potato wedges are added, mix them to coat them thoroughly.

4. Set the air fryer to 400°F.

5. Ensure that the potato wedges are arranged in the air fryer basket in a single layer, free of any contact.

6. Cook until golden brown and crispy, shaking the basket or rotating the wedges halfway through, 20 to 25 minutes.

7. Once the wedges are cooked through, transfer them to a platter and garnish with Parmesan cheese, fresh parsley, and sea salt, if desired.

Air Fryer Coconut Shrimp with Dipping Sauce

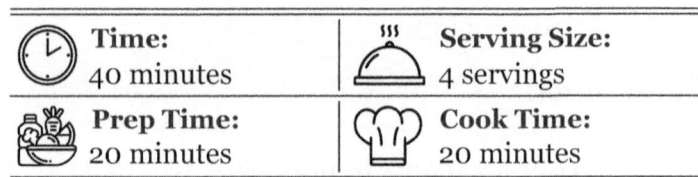

Nutrition Information:

Calories: 375, Fat: 10g, Total Carbohydrate: 45g, Protein: 25g, Sodium: 930mg.

Ingredients:

- 1 lb large shrimp, peeled and deveined
- 1/2 cup all-purpose flour
- 1 tsp salt
- 1/2 tsp black pepper
- 2 large eggs, beaten
- 1 cup unsweetened shredded coconut
- 1/2 cup panko bread crumbs
- Cooking spray
- For the Dipping Sauce:
- 1/2 cup orange marmalade
- 1 tbsp freshly squeezed lime juice

- 1 tsp soy sauce
- 1/4 tsp crushed red pepper flakes

Directions:

1. Preheat your air fryer to 400°F (200°C).
2. Transfer the flour into a bowl and season with salt and pepper. Place the beaten eggs into a different bowl, and in a third bowl, combine the panko bread crumbs and the shredded coconut.
3. After dipping each prawn in the flour mixture, beaten eggs, and eggs, coat it well with the coconut-panko mixture. To ensure the mixture adheres to the prawns, firmly press it onto them.
4. Make sure the coated prawns are layered in the air fryer basket without coming into contact with one another. Applying cooking spray to the prawns should be done sparingly.
5. They should be crispy and golden after 12 to 15 minutes of cooking in the air fryer, with a midway flip.
6. While the shrimp are cooking, prepare the dipping sauce by combining the marmalade, lime juice, soy sauce, and red pepper flakes in a basin. Stir to fully combine.
7. Present the warm, crispy shrimp alongside the accompanying dipping sauce.

Light & Fluffy Air Fryer Donuts

Time: 1 hour 5 minutes	Serving Size: 4 servings
Prep Time: 25 minutes	Cook Time: 40 minutes

Nutrition Information:

Calories: 145, Fat: 4g, Total Carbohydrate: 25g, Protein: 3g, Sodium: 140mg.

Ingredients:

- 1 cup all-purpose flour
- 3 tbsp granulated sugar
- 1 tsp baking powder
- 1/4 tsp salt
- 1/4 cup low-fat milk
- 1 large egg
- 2 tbsp unsalted butter, melted
- 1 tsp pure vanilla extract
- Cooking spray
- Optional: Powdered sugar for dusting

Directions:

1. Mix the flour, salt, baking soda, and granulated sugar in a sizable mixing bowl.
2. Melted butter, milk, egg, and vanilla essence are combined separately.
3. A soft dough will develop after adding the wet components to the dry ones and stirring.
4. On a floured surface, roll out the dough to about 1/2-inch thickness. Use a donut or a large and small round cutter to cut out donut shapes.
5. Set your air fryer's temperature to 350°F (175°C).
6. Please ensure the donuts are arranged in the air fryer basket in a single layer without touching them. Cooking spray should be lightly applied to the tops.
7. Flip halfway through cooking in the air fryer for 12 to 15 minutes or until golden brown.
8. Allow the donuts to cool slightly, and dust with powdered sugar if desired.
9. Serve warm and enjoy!

Chapter 14: 30-Day Meal Prep Plan

Week 1

Day 1:

Breakfast: Israeli Sabich Sandwich

Snack 1: Spinach and Feta Stuffed Mushrooms

Lunch: Mediterranean Veggie Pizza

Snack 2: Hummus and Veggie Sticks

Dinner: Mediterranean Fish Stew

Dessert: Pistachio Pudding with Saffron

Beverage: Lemon and Mint Cooler

Day 2:

Breakfast: Cilbir: Turkish Poached Eggs with Yogurt Sauce

Snack 1: Greek Salad Skewers

Lunch: Cucumber Yogurt Salad (Tzatziki) with pita bread

Snack 2: Marinated Olives and Feta

Dinner: Mediterranean Pork Tenderloin with Olives and Feta

Dessert: Mediterranean Date Balls with Coconut

Beverage: Iced Hibiscus and Rose Tea

Day 3:

Breakfast: Mediterranean Egg Muffins with Zucchini and Sun-dried Tomatoes

Snack 1: Mediterranean Bruschetta

Lunch: Tabbouleh

Snack 2: Baba Ganoush with sliced cucumbers

Dinner: Garlic Rosemary Roasted Chicken

Dessert: Fig and Walnut Halva

Beverage: Olive Leaf Tea

Day 4:

Breakfast: Lemon Ricotta Pancakes with Blueberries

Snack 1: Caponata Crostini

Lunch: Tomato and Basil Soup

Snack 2: Baba Ganoush with carrot sticks

Dinner: Tuscan Chicken with Tomatoes and Spinach

Dessert: Fig and Walnut Halva

Beverage: Fresh Pomegranate and Orange Juice

Day 5:

Breakfast: Lemon Ricotta Pancakes with Blueberries

Snack 1: Caponata Crostini

Lunch: Fennel and Orange Salad

Snack 2: Spinach and Feta Stuffed Mushrooms

Dinner: Beef and Eggplant Moussaka

Dessert: Mediterranean Almond Cookies

Beverage: Greek Mountain Tea with Lemon and Honey

Day 6:

Breakfast: Mediterranean Breakfast Wrap

Snack 1: Tzatziki Dip with a side of carrots

Lunch: Mediterranean Beet Salad

Snack 2: Greek Salad Skewers

Dinner: Chicken Kebabs with Tzatziki Sauce

Dessert: Baklava Rolls with Pistachio and Honey

Beverage: Mediterranean Iced Coffee with Almond Milk

Day 7:

Breakfast: Greek Yogurt Parfait with Honey and Berries

Snack 1: Hummus and Veggie Sticks

Lunch: Chickpea and Roasted Pepper Salad

Snack 2: Muhammara

Dinner: Garlic Lemon Herb Grilled Salmon

Dessert: Mediterranean Lemon Olive Oil Cake

Beverage: Fresh Pomegranate and Orange Juice

Week 2

Day 8:

Breakfast: Mediterranean Breakfast Wrap

Snack 1: Mediterranean Bruschetta

Lunch: Lentil and Roasted Carrot Salad

Snack 2: Greek Salad Skewers

Dinner: Spiced Pork Kebabs with Cucumber Salad

Dessert: Orange and Rose Water Sorbet

Beverage: Mediterranean Iced Coffee with Almond Milk

Day 9:

Breakfast: Greek Yogurt Parfait with Honey and Berries

Snack 1: Tzatziki Dip

Lunch: Cretan Tomato Soup with Orzo

Snack 2: Marinated Olives and Feta

Dinner: Baked Sardines with Lemon and Oregano

Dessert: Mediterranean Date Balls with Coconut

Beverage: Sparkling Rosemary Limeade

Day 10:

Breakfast: Turkish Menemen with Bell Peppers

Snack 1: Greek Salad Skewers

Lunch: Mediterranean Vegetable Soup

Snack 2: Muhammara with whole grain crackers

Dinner: Mediterranean Turkey Burgers

Dessert: Baklava Rolls with Pistachio and Honey

Beverage: Greek Frappe Coffee

Day 11:

Breakfast: Turkish Menemen with Bell Peppers

Snack 1: Marinated Olives

Lunch: Za'atar Roasted Carrots and Lemon Herb Orzo Salad

Snack 2: Falafel Bites with Tzatziki Dip

Dinner: Greek-style Shrimp Pasta

Dessert: Apricot and Almond Tart

Beverage: Sparkling Rosemary Limeade

Day 12:

Breakfast: Cilbir: Turkish Poached Eggs with Yogurt Sauce

Snack 1: Spinach and Feta Stuffed Mushrooms

Lunch: Garlic Sautéed Green Beans and Fennel and Orange Salad

Snack 2: Marinated Olives

Dinner: Beef Kofta with Yogurt Sauce

Dessert: Mediterranean Almond Cookies

Beverage: Lemon and Mint Cooler

Day 13:

Breakfast: Mediterranean Overnight Oats with Apricots and Pistachios

Snack 1: Tzatziki Dip with fresh cucumber slices

Lunch: Chickpea and Spinach Stew

Snack 2: Falafel Bites
Dinner: Easy Cod in Tomato Basil Sauce
Dessert: Mediterranean Lemon Olive Oil Cake
Beverage: Mediterranean Herbal Tea Blend

Day 14:
Breakfast: Greek Avocado Toast with Kalamata Olives
Snack 1: Hummus and Veggie Sticks
Lunch: Lentil and Spinach Soup
Snack 2: Mediterranean Bruschetta
Dinner: Grilled Lamb Chops with Mint Sauce
Dessert: Fresh Fruit Salad with Mint and Lemon Drizzle
Beverage: Mint and Cucumber Infused Water

Week 3

Day 15:
Breakfast: Turkish Menemen with Bell Peppers
Snack 1: Muhammara
Lunch: Chickpea and Roasted Pepper Salad
Snack 2: Caponata Crostini
Dinner: Spiced Chicken with Couscous Salad
Dessert: Mediterranean Almond Cookies
Beverage: Sparkling Rosemary Limeade

Day 16:
Breakfast: Greek Avocado Toast with Kalamata Olives
Snack 1: Falafel Bites
Lunch: Mediterranean Beet Salad with Za'atar Roasted Carrots
Snack 2: Marinated Olives and Feta
Dinner: Mediterranean Fish Stew with Potatoes and Olives
Dessert: Greek Yogurt with Honey and Walnuts
Beverage: Greek Mountain Tea with Lemon and Honey

Day 17:
Breakfast: Mediterranean Breakfast Wrap
Snack 1: Tzatziki Dip with veggie sticks
Lunch: Escarole and White Bean Soup
Snack 2: Baba Ganoush with pita bread

Dinner: Lamb Tagine with Dates and Cinnamon

Dessert: Pistachio Pudding with Saffron

Beverage: Olive Leaf Tea

Day 18:

Breakfast: Israeli Sabich Sandwich

Snack 1: Falafel Bites

Lunch: Creamy Butternut Squash Soup (from Bonus Chapter)

Snack 2: Baba Ganoush with Pita Bread

Dinner: Garlic Lemon Herb Grilled Salmon

Dessert: Mediterranean Date Balls with Coconut

Beverage: Lemon and Mint Cooler

Day 19:

Breakfast: Israeli Sabich Sandwich

Snack 1: Mediterranean Bruschetta

Lunch: Chickpea and Spinach Stew with Lemon Herb Orzo Salad

Snack 2: Caponata Crostini

Dinner: Mediterranean Chicken Salad with Olives and Feta

Dessert: Baklava Rolls with Pistachio and Honey

Beverage: Mint and Cucumber Infused Water

Day 20:

Breakfast: Cilbir: Turkish Poached Eggs with Yogurt Sauce

Snack 1: Marinated Olives

Lunch: Mediterranean Vegetable Soup

Snack 2: Greek Salad Skewers

Dinner: Beef and Eggplant Moussaka

Dessert: Mediterranean Lemon Olive Oil Cake

Beverage: Iced Hibiscus and Rose Tea

Day 21:

Breakfast: Mediterranean Overnight Oats with Apricots and Pistachios

Snack 1: Muhammara with whole grain pita chips

Lunch: Mediterranean Cucumber and Tomato Salad with Pesto Fusilli with Cherry Tomatoes

Snack 2: Spinach and Feta Stuffed Mushrooms

Dinner: Chicken Kebabs with Tzatziki Sauce

Dessert: Apricot and Almond Tart

Beverage: Lemon and Mint Cooler

Week 4

Day 22:

Breakfast: Mediterranean Overnight Oats with Apricots and Pistachios

Snack 1: Spinach and Feta Stuffed Mushrooms

Lunch: Pesto Fusilli with Cherry Tomatoes

Snack 2: Muhammara with whole grain crackers

Dinner: Lamb Tagine with Dates and Cinnamon

Dessert: Fresh Fruit Salad with Mint and Lemon Drizzle

Beverage: Greek Mountain Tea with Lemon and Honey

Day 23:

Breakfast: Greek Avocado Toast with Kalamata Olives

Snack 1: Marinated Olives

Lunch: Air-Fried Parmesan Zucchini Sticks (from Bonus Chapter)

Snack 2: Tzatziki Dip with pita bread

Dinner: Mediterranean Chicken Salad with Olives and Feta

Dessert: Pistachio Pudding with Saffron

Beverage: Mint and Cucumber Infused Water

Day 24:

Breakfast: Lemon Ricotta Pancakes with Blueberries

Snack 1: Caponata Crostini

Lunch: Mediterranean Vegetable Soup

Snack 2: Hummus and Veggie Sticks

Dinner: Beef Kofta with Yogurt Sauce

Dessert: Greek Yogurt with Honey and Walnuts

Beverage: Sparkling Rosemary Limeade

Day 25:

Breakfast: Turkish Menemen with Bell Peppers

Snack 1: Marinated Olives and Feta

Lunch: Zucchini and Ricotta Galette

Snack 2: Greek Salad Skewers

Dinner: Slow-cooked Pork Shoulder with Mediterranean Herbs

Dessert: Baklava Rolls with Pistachio and Honey

Beverage: Mediterranean Iced Coffee with Almond Milk

Day 26:

Breakfast: Lemon Ricotta Pancakes with Blueberries

Snack 1: Hummus and Veggie Sticks

Lunch: Tomato and Basil Soup

Snack 2: Spinach and Feta Stuffed Mushrooms

Dinner: Olive and Caper Anchovy Pasta

Dessert: Mediterranean Date Balls with Coconut

Beverage: Mediterranean Iced Coffee with Almond Milk

Day 27:

Breakfast: Cilbir: Turkish Poached Eggs with Yogurt Sauce

Snack 1: Mediterranean Bruschetta

Lunch: Honey Garlic Chicken with Carrots and Broccoli (from Bonus Chapter)

Snack 2: Spinach and Feta Stuffed Mushrooms

Dinner: Mediterranean Tuna Salad

Dessert: Mediterranean Lemon Olive Oil Cake

Beverage: Greek Frappe Coffee

Day 28:

Breakfast: Mediterranean Overnight Oats with Apricots and Pistachios

Snack 1: Tzatziki Dip with Veggie Sticks

Lunch: Chickpea and Rosemary Soup

Snack 2: Muhammara with pita chips

Dinner: Tuscan Chicken with Tomatoes and Spinach

Dessert: Apricot and Almond Tart

Beverage: Iced Hibiscus and Rose Tea

Day 29:

Breakfast: Mediterranean Egg Muffins with Zucchini and Sun-dried Tomatoes

Snack 1: Spinach and Feta Stuffed Mushrooms

Lunch: Mediterranean Veggie Pizza

Snack 2: Marinated Olives

Dinner: Spiced Pork Kebabs with Cucumber Salad

Dessert: Fig and Walnut Halva

Beverage: Mediterranean Herbal Tea Blend

Day 30:

Breakfast: Greek Yogurt Parfait with Honey and Berries

Snack 1: Hummus and Veggie Sticks

Lunch: Quinoa & Vegetable Medley Salad (from Bonus Chapter)

Snack 2: Greek Salad Skewers

Dinner: Greek-style Stuffed Bell Peppers with Ground Lamb

Dessert: Orange and Rose Water Sorbet

Beverage: Fresh Pomegranate and Orange Juice

Free Gift

Thank you! Discover your gift inside! Dive into a rich assortment of DASH Diet for Beginners recipes for added inspiration. Gift it or share the PDF effortlessly with friends and family via a single click on WhatsApp or other social platforms. Bon appétit!

Conclusion outline

The Mediterranean diet is a celebration of life, flavors, and well-being rather than merely a set of dietary rules. This diet isn't about deprivation or calculating calories; instead, it was inspired by the eating habits of nations nested around the Mediterranean Sea. It's about embracing nutritious foods, in-season produce, and bold flavors that boost your immune system and satisfy your appetite.

Diets that promise immediate results but frequently result in long-term health concerns are easy to fall victim to in our fast-paced world, where convenience frequently takes precedence over quality. Sugars, bad fats, and processed foods abound in the average modern diet. Over time, a diet like that can deprive our bodies of vital nutrients and pave the way for many health problems. This is where the Mediterranean diet's beauty shines. With an emphasis on whole foods, lean proteins, healthy fats, and an abundance of fruits and vegetables, this diet meets your body's nutritional requirements and makes sure it thrives.

Making the switch to a Mediterranean diet entails deciding to live a long, healthy life where you enjoy every meal. The advantages are numerous, ranging from improving heart health to lowering the risk of chronic illnesses to helping with weight management. Beyond its health benefits, this diet, which is modeled after the Mediterranean way of life, also encourages mental clarity and emotional equilibrium.

As you explore the recipes and recommendations inside this book, keep in mind that following a Mediterranean diet does not need perfection; instead, it requires development. One meal at a time, wiser decisions must be made. You'll notice a change in your health and a greater appreciation for the basic pleasures of delicious food as you gradually immerse yourself in the tastes and rhythms of this diet.

We have tried to give you thorough guidance to start your Mediterranean adventure in this book. We hope that our abundance of recipes covering a variety of meals and occasions, together with a sample four-week meal plan, will make your transition easier and more pleasurable.

Recall that your tour of the Mediterranean is far from over when you end this chapter. The versatility and durability of the Mediterranean diet are its key components. Thus, adapt to it, try new things, and, most of all, have fun while doing it.

A modest request before you set out on your culinary travels. Please take the time to share your thoughts on whether this book has improved your life, helped you make healthier decisions, or just exposed you to a new favorite food. A review on [name of platform] would be very valuable. Your advice will not only assist us in becoming better, but it will also assist other readers when they travel the Mediterranean.

We are grateful that you have chosen this route of health and flavor. Cheers to a better, happier self and bon appétit!

References

Mediterranean Diet Foundation. (2023). The Mediterranean Diet. https://www.mediterraneandietfoundation.com/

Oldways Preservation Trust. (2023). Mediterranean Diet. https://oldwayspt.org/traditional-diets/mediterranean-diet

Harvard T.H. Chan School of Public Health. (2023). The Nutrition Source: Mediterranean Diet. https://www.hsph.harvard.edu/nutritionsource/healthy-eating-plate/

American Heart Association. (2023). Mediterranean Diet. https://www.heart.org/en/healthy-living/healthy-eating/eat-smart/nutrition-basics/mediterranean-diet

Mayo Clinic. (2023). Mediterranean Diet: A Heart-Healthy Eating Plan. https://www.mayoclinic.org/healthy-lifestyle/nutrition-and-healthy-eating/in-depth/mediterranean-diet/art-20047801

The Mediterranean Dish. (2023). Mediterranean Recipes. https://www.themediterraneandish.com/

Epicurious. (2023). Mediterranean Diet Recipes. https://www.epicurious.com/special-consideration/mediterranean

Cooking Light. (2023). Mediterranean Diet Meal Plans. https://www.cookinglight.com/eating-smart/nutrition-101/mediterranean-diet-meal-plans

Mediterranean Living. (2023). Mediterranean Diet Recipes and Lifestyle. https://www.mediterraneanliving.com/

World Health Organization. (2023). Healthy Diet. https://www.who.int/news-room/fact-sheets/detail/healthy-diet

Appendix 1: Measurement Conversion Chart

U.S. System	Metric
1 inch	2.54 centimeters
1 fluid ounce	29.57 milliliters
1 pint (16 ounces)	473.18 milliliters, 2 cups
1 quart (32 ounces)	1 liter, 4 cups
1 gallon (128 ounces)	4 liters, 16 cups
1 pound (16 ounces)	437.5 grams (0.4536 kilogram), 473.18 milliliters
1 ounces	2 tablespoons, 28 grams
1 cup (8 ounces)	237 milliliters
1 teaspoon	5 milliliters
1 tablespoon	15 milliliters (3 teaspoons)
Fahrenheit (subtract 32 and divide by 1.8 to get Celsius)	Centigrade (multiply by 1.8 and add 32 to get Fahrenheit)

Appendix 2: Index Recipes

A

Almonds

Mediterranean Almond Cookies - **82**

Apricot and Almond Tart - **83**

Baklava Rolls with Pistachio and Honey - **82**

Pistachio Pudding with Saffron - **85**

Mediterranean Date Balls with Coconut - **85**

Almond Berry Overnight Oats - **95**

Fig and Walnut Halva - **84**

Asparagus

Eggplant and Bell Pepper Caponata - **51**

Beef and Eggplant Moussaka - **73**

Avocado

Greek Avocado Toast with Kalamata Olives - **20**

B

Basil

Tomato and Mozzarella Farfalle - **44**

Tomato and Basil Soup - **37**

Margherita Flatbread Pizza - **45**

Tomato and Olive Rice Salad - **48**

Mediterranean Veggie Pizza - **45**

Pesto Fusilli with Cherry Tomatoes - **43**

Easy Cod in Tomato Basil Sauce - **59**

DASH-friendly Whole Wheat Spaghetti with Fresh Tomato Sauce - **95**

Beef

Beef and Eggplant Moussaka - **73**

Mediterranean Beef Stew with Rosemary and Tomatoes - **77**

Beef Kofta with Yogurt Sauce - **75**

Spiced Pork Kebabs with Cucumber Salad - **76**

Slow-cooked Pork Shoulder with Mediterranean Herbs - **78**

Greek-style Stuffed Bell Peppers with Ground Lamb - **75**

Beetroot

Mediterranean Beet Salad - **30**

Bell Peppers

Turkish Menemen with Bell Peppers - **17**

Mediterranean Breakfast Wrap - **15**

Eggplant and Bell Pepper Caponata - **51**

Stuffed Bell Peppers with Quinoa and Feta - **53**

Mediterranean Fish Stew with Potatoes and Olives - **62**

Greek-style Shrimp Pasta - **62**

Spiced Chicken with Couscous Salad - **67**

Blueberries

Lemon Ricotta Pancakes with Blueberries - **16**

Broccoli

Roasted Broccoli with Lemon and Garlic - **54**

Honey Garlic Chicken with Carrots and Broccoli - **96**

C

Carrots

Za'atar Roasted Carrots - **34**

Lentil and Roasted Carrot Salad - **52**

Honey Garlic Chicken with Carrots and Broccoli - **96**

Mediterranean Vegetable Soup - **40**

Chickpeas

Hummus and Veggie Sticks - **23**

Chickpea and Roasted Pepper Salad - **29**

Chickpea and Spinach Stew - **50**

Chickpea and Rosemary Soup - **36**

Escarole and White Bean Soup - **40**

Crockpot Vegetable and Bean Chili - **97**

Cucumber

Cucumber Yogurt Salad (Tzatziki) - **33**

Mediterranean Cucumber and Tomato Salad - **52**

Greek Yogurt Parfait with Honey and Berries - **15**

Cretan Tomato Soup with Orzo - **41**

Spiced Pork Kebabs with Cucumber Salad - **76**

Greek Yogurt with Honey and Walnuts - **80**

Mint and Cucumber Infused Water - **87**

D

Dill

Greek Yogurt with Honey and Walnuts - **80**

F

Fennel

Fennel and Orange Salad - **30**

Seared Scallops with Fennel Salad - **61**

Feta

Greek Salad Skewers - **25**

Roasted Red Pepper and Feta Spread - **31**

Spinach and Feta Stuffed Mushrooms - **27**

Marinated Olives and Feta - **32**

Mediterranean Chicken Salad with Olives and Feta - **70**

Stuffed Bell Peppers with Quinoa and Feta - **53**

Mediterranean Pork Tenderloin with Olives and Feta - **73**

Fig

Fig and Walnut Halva - **84**

Fish

Mediterranean Fish Stew with Potatoes and Olives - **62**

Greek Lemon Chicken Soup (Avgolemono) - **38**

Baked Tilapia with Tomatoes and Olives - **58**

Greek-style Shrimp Pasta - **62**

Easy Cod in Tomato Basil Sauce - **59**

Mussels in White Wine and Garlic Sauce - **59**

Olive and Caper Anchovy Pasta - **60**

Baked Sardines with Lemon and Oregano - **60**

Seared Scallops with Fennel Salad - **61**

Spinach and Feta Stuffed Tilapia - **94**

G

Garlic

Lemon Herb Orzo Salad - **34**

Mediterranean Vegetable Soup - **40**

Gazpacho

Tomato and Mozzarella Farfalle - **44**

Margherita Flatbread Pizza - **45**

Mediterranean Veggie Pizza - **45**

Chicken and Pesto Pizza - **46**

Saffron and Vegetable Pilaf - **48**

Zucchini and Ricotta Galette - **49**

Garlic Sautéed Green Beans - **50**

Chickpea and Spinach Stew - **50**

Lentil and Roasted Carrot Salad - **52**

Braised Cannellini Beans with Kale - **54**

Roasted Broccoli with Lemon and Garlic - **54**

Garlic Lemon Herb Grilled Salmon - **57**

Baked Tilapia with Tomatoes and Olives - **58**

Mussels in White Wine and Garlic Sauce - **59**

Seared Scallops with Fennel Salad - **61**

Mediterranean Fish Stew with Potatoes and Olives - **62**

Chicken Kebabs with Tzatziki Sauce - **65**

Garlic Rosemary Roasted Chicken - **69**

Mediterranean Chicken Salad with Olives and Feta - **70**

Chicken Tagine with Apricots and Almonds - **65**

Tuscan Chicken with Tomatoes and Spinach - **66**

Spiced Chicken with Couscous Salad - **67**

Lemon Olive Chicken Thighs - **69**

Mediterranean Beef Stew with Rosemary and Tomatoes - **77**

Lamb and Spinach Curry - **77**

Slow-cooked Pork Shoulder with Mediterranean Herbs - **78**

Greek Yogurt with Honey and Walnuts - **80**

Honey Garlic Chicken with Carrots and Broccoli - **96**

Air-Fried Parmesan Zucchini Sticks - **99**

Green Beans

Garlic Sautéed Green Beans - **50**

H

Herbs

Lemon Herb Orzo Salad - **34**

Za'atar Roasted Carrots - **34**

Mediterranean Vegetable Soup - **40**

Greek Lemon Chicken Soup (Avgolemono) - **38**

Mediterranean Fish Stew with Potatoes and Olives - **62**

Lemon Olive Chicken Thighs - **69**

Mediterranean Chicken Salad with Olives and Feta - **70**

Garlic Lemon Herb Grilled Salmon - **57**

Chicken Kebabs with Tzatziki Sauce - **65**

Garlic Rosemary Roasted Chicken - **69**

Slow-cooked Pork Shoulder with Mediterranean Herbs - **78**

Mediterranean Beef Stew with Rosemary and Tomatoes - **77**

Beef Kofta with Yogurt Sauce - **75**

Spiced Pork Kebabs with Cucumber Salad - **76**

Lamb and Spinach Curry - **77**

Air-Fried Parmesan Zucchini Sticks - **99**

Mint and Cucumber Infused Water - **87**

Honey

Mediterranean Date Balls with Coconut - **85**

Baklava Rolls with Pistachio and Honey - **82**

Pistachio Pudding with Saffron - **85**

Greek Yogurt Parfait with Honey and Berries - **15**

Greek Yogurt with Honey and Walnuts - **80**

K

Kale

Lentil and Roasted Carrot Salad - **52**

Braised Cannellini Beans with Kale - **54**

Kalamata Olives

Greek Salad Skewers - **25**

Greek Avocado Toast with Kalamata Olives - **20**

Tomato and Olive Rice Salad - **48**

Mediterranean Veggie Pizza - **45**

Mediterranean Chicken Salad with Olives and Feta - **70**

Mediterranean Pork Tenderloin with Olives and Feta - **73**

Baked Tilapia with Tomatoes and Olives - **58**

Mediterranean Fish Stew with Potatoes and Olives - **62**

L

Lamb

Lamb and Spinach Curry - **77**

Greek-style Stuffed Bell Peppers with Ground Lamb - **75**

Beef Kofta with Yogurt Sauce - **75**

Leek

Mediterranean Vegetable Soup - **40**

Lemon

Lemon Herb Orzo Salad - **34**

Greek Lemon Chicken Soup (Avgolemono) - **38**

Cretan Tomato Soup with Orzo - **41**

Lemon Olive Chicken Thighs - 69

Garlic Lemon Herb Grilled Salmon - 57

Spiced Chicken with Couscous Salad - 67

Greek Yogurt with Honey and Walnuts - 80

Lentils

Lentil and Roasted Carrot Salad - 52

M

Mint

Mediterranean Date Balls with Coconut - 85

Greek Yogurt Parfait with Honey and Berries - 15

Mediterranean Vegetable Soup - 40

Mediterranean Veggie Pizza - 45

Zucchini and Ricotta Galette - 49

Mediterranean Fish Stew with Potatoes and Olives - 62

Mediterranean Chicken Salad with Olives and Feta - 70

Spiced Chicken with Couscous Salad - 67

Mediterranean Beef Stew with Rosemary and Tomatoes - 77

Spiced Pork Kebabs with Cucumber Salad - 76

Slow-cooked Pork Shoulder with Mediterranean Herbs - 78

Lamb and Spinach Curry - 77

Mint and Cucumber Infused Water - 87

Mozzarella

Tomato and Mozzarella Farfalle - 44

Mediterranean Veggie Pizza - 45

Margherita Flatbread Pizza - 45

Mushrooms

Spinach and Feta Stuffed Mushrooms - 27

Mussels

Mediterranean Fish Stew with Potatoes and Olives - 62

Mussels in White Wine and Garlic Sauce - 59

O

Olives

Greek Salad Skewers - 25

Greek Avocado Toast with Kalamata Olives - 20

Marinated Olives and Feta - 32

Mediterranean Chicken Salad with Olives and Feta - 70

Mediterranean Pork Tenderloin with Olives and Feta - 73

Mediterranean Veggie Pizza - 45

Mediterranean Fish Stew with Potatoes and Olives - 62

Tomato and Olive Rice Salad - 48

Baked Tilapia with Tomatoes and Olives - 58

Orzo

Lemon Herb Orzo Salad - 34

Cretan Tomato Soup with Orzo - 41

P

Parmesan

Mediterranean Veggie Pizza - 45

Margherita Flatbread Pizza - 45

Pesto Fusilli with Cherry Tomatoes - 43

Mediterranean Fish Stew with Potatoes and Olives - 62

Mediterranean Pork Tenderloin with Olives and Feta - 73

Zucchini and Ricotta Galette - 49

Air-Fried Parmesan Zucchini Sticks - 99

Pasta

Tomato and Mozzarella Farfalle - 44

Pesto Fusilli with Cherry Tomatoes - 43

DASH-friendly Whole Wheat Spaghetti with Fresh Tomato Sauce - 95

Olive and Caper Anchovy Pasta - 60

Greek-style Shrimp Pasta - 62

Peppers

Turkish Menemen with Bell Peppers - 17

Mediterranean Breakfast Wrap - 15

Greek-style Stuffed Bell Peppers with Ground Lamb - 75

Mediterranean Fish Stew with Potatoes and Olives - 62

Greek-style Shrimp Pasta - 62

Spiced Chicken with Couscous Salad - 67

Stuffed Bell Peppers with Quinoa and Feta - 53

Eggplant and Bell Pepper Caponata - 51

Roasted Red Pepper and Feta Spread - 31

Marinated Olives and Feta - 32

Pistachios

Mediterranean Almond Cookies - 82

Baklava Rolls with Pistachio and Honey - 82

Pistachio Pudding with Saffron - 85

Potatoes

Mediterranean Vegetable Soup - 40

Mediterranean Fish Stew with Potatoes and Olives - 62

Greek-style Stuffed Bell Peppers with Ground Lamb - 75

Greek Lemon Chicken Soup (Avgolemono) - 38

Chicken and Pesto Pizza - 46

Pesto Fusilli with Cherry Tomatoes - 43

Spiced Pork Kebabs with Cucumber Salad - 76

Crockpot Vegetable and Bean Chili - 97

Mediterranean Beef Stew with Rosemary and Tomatoes - 77

Q

Quinoa

Greek-style Stuffed Bell Peppers with Ground Lamb - 75

Stuffed Bell Peppers with Quinoa and Feta - 53

R

Ricotta

Zucchini and Ricotta Galette - 49

Rice

Tomato and Olive Rice Salad - 48

Rosemary

Mediterranean Vegetable Soup - 40

Mediterranean Fish Stew with Potatoes and Olives - 62

Pesto Fusilli with Cherry Tomatoes - 43

Mediterranean Chicken Salad with Olives and Feta - 70

Mediterranean Pork Tenderloin with Olives and Feta - 73

Garlic Rosemary Roasted Chicken - 69

Slow-cooked Pork Shoulder with Mediterranean Herbs - 78

Mediterranean Beef Stew with Rosemary and Tomatoes - 77

S

Salmon

Garlic Lemon Herb Grilled Salmon - 57

Mediterranean Fish Stew with Potatoes and Olives - 62

Greek-style Shrimp Pasta - 62

Lemon Herb Orzo Salad - 34

Saffron

Pistachio Pudding with Saffron - 85

Seafood

Mediterranean Fish Stew with Potatoes and Olives - 62

Mussels in White Wine and Garlic Sauce - 59

Greek-style Shrimp Pasta - 62

Spinach

Lamb and Spinach Curry - 77

Greek-style Stuffed Bell Peppers with Ground Lamb - 75

Mediterranean Vegetable Soup - 40

Mediterranean Chicken Salad with Olives and Feta - 70

Spinach and Feta Stuffed Mushrooms - 27

Stuffed Bell Peppers with Quinoa and Feta - 53

Squash

Greek-style Stuffed Bell Peppers with Ground Lamb - 75

Mediterranean Vegetable Soup - 40

T

Thyme

Mediterranean Vegetable Soup - 40

Mediterranean Chicken Salad with Olives and Feta - 70

Mediterranean Pork Tenderloin with Olives and Feta - 73

Lemon Olive Chicken Thighs - 69

Garlic Rosemary Roasted Chicken - 69

Slow-cooked Pork Shoulder with Mediterranean Herbs - 78

Tomatoes

Greek-style Stuffed Bell Peppers with Ground Lamb - 75

Mediterranean Vegetable Soup - 40

Mediterranean Fish Stew with Potatoes and Olives - 62

Tomato and Mozzarella Farfalle - 44

Mediterranean Chicken Salad with Olives and Feta - 70

Greek-style Shrimp Pasta - 62

Spiced Chicken with Couscous Salad - 67

Tomato and Olive Rice Salad - 48

Baked Tilapia with Tomatoes and Olives - 58

Pesto Fusilli with Cherry Tomatoes - 43

Cretan Tomato Soup with Orzo - 41

DASH-friendly Whole Wheat Spaghetti with Fresh Tomato Sauce - 95

Crockpot Vegetable and Bean Chili - 97

Olive and Caper Anchovy Pasta - 60

Marinated Olives and Feta - 32

Greek Salad Skewers - 25

Eggplant and Bell Pepper Caponata - 51

Roasted Red Pepper and Feta Spread - 31

W

Walnuts

Mediterranean Almond Cookies - 82

Mediterranean Date Balls with Coconut - 85

Baklava Rolls with Pistachio and Honey - 82

Z

Zucchini

Zucchini and Ricotta Galette - 49

Mediterranean Veggie Pizza - 45

Mediterranean Vegetable Soup - 40

Air-Fried Parmesan Zucchini Sticks - 99

Notes

Printed in Great Britain
by Amazon